VAMPIRES

MONSTERS OF TRUE CRIME

BEN OAKLEY

WELVETREES

CAMDEN

TITLES BY BEN OAKLEY

FICTION

HARRISON LAKE INVESTIGATIONS
The Camden Killer
The Limehouse Hotel
Monster of the Algarve

HONEYSUCKLE GOODWILLIES
The Mystery of Grimlow Forest
The Mystery of Crowstones Island

SUBNET SF TRILOGY
Unknown Origin
Alien Network
Final Contact

NONFICTION

TRUE CRIME
Bizarre True Crime Series
Monsters of True Crime
Orrible British True Crime Series
The Monstrous Book of Serial Killers
True Crime 365 series
Year of the Serial Killer

OTHER NONFICTION
The Immortal Hour: The True Story of Netta Fornario
Suicide Prevention Handbook

'I sawed off his head so that the children would make fun of him when he arrived in heaven.'

The Vampire of Niterói.

ISBN: 978-1-915929-07-5

Cover design by Ben Oakley. Images by Marina Luisa.

For information about special discounts available
for bulk purchases, sales promotions, book signings,
trade shows, and distribution, contact
hello@twelvetreescamden.co.uk

Twelvetrees Camden Ltd
71-75 Shelton Street, Covent Garden
London, WC2H 9JQ

www.twelvetreescamden.co.uk

VAMPIRES: MONSTERS OF TRUE CRIME

Vampires: Monsters of True Crime 7

Drained of Blood on Walpurgis Night..................................... 19

Countess Dracula.. 29

Soul Eater and the Runaway Devil... 43

The Vampire Clan Murders... 55

The Nuremberg Vampire 65

Vampire of Anglesey.. 75

Vampire of Sacramento.. 85

The Brazilian Blood-Drinker... 95

Vampire Killer Couple 105

Vampire of Hanover 117

Marshfield Vampire Killer... 131

Kiss of the Vampire.. 139

The Scottish Vampire 149

The Lesbian Vampire Killer 159

The Vampire Rapist 171

Bonus: Bizarre True Crime Preview 183

VAMPIRES: MONSTERS OF TRUE CRIME

There is perhaps nothing more everlasting than the image of the vampire chomping down on the neck of an innocent girl. A romanticism is often found at the heart of the lore, but as this book shows, real vampires are not all shimmering lights and deep kisses. They are brutal, violent, hungry for blood, and oh so very real.

But first, a warning.

Due to the nature of this book and the subject it discusses, there are depictions of self-harm included in some of the stories. **This is from the outset of this book.** If you self-harm or are thinking of self-harming then throw this book in the bin.

Literally, throw it in the bin! Now!

If you feel your mental health is in a strong enough place to read the real-life horrors within and you are aware of what real-life vampire killers likely do, then let us proceed.

Curse of real-world vampirism.

My first run-in with real-world vampires was back in 1996, when I was an old world-weary teenager. Vampirism had become a sub-culture associated with the alternative crowds. Everyone seemed to have their cutting packs or hideaway pockets, either for drug use or self-harm actuation.

Some would cut themselves because of deep emotional turmoil, others for a sense of belonging. There were a few that would even cut themselves because it was considered fun, or they believed themselves vampiric in nature.

I remember walking down a stairway from an underground rock club to get to the toilets. When I reached the corridor, it was black and long, as if a tunnel of degradation extended away from me into a black nothingness.

It was covered in old gig posters that had been tortured and ripped at for a decade, a testament to the throwaway culture of the age. It was always crowded with people lining the walls, soul-searching, smooching – and bloodletting.

No one hid their bloodletting because it was morally and culturally acceptable. There were a few groans from those who had birthed the genre in the seventies, but no help was suggested. No one reached out and told them it was wrong, in fact no one reached out at all.

Self-harm was their friend, however horrific that sounds today. I was part of a lost generation, caught in a moment of time that would become the final stage of the second millennium of human history.

The only people that did reach out were those who believed that cutting served more of a purpose, more than simply self-harm. That vampiric tendency I mentioned up above was all too prevalent among that culture.

I'm not one to discuss the fallacies of the existence of mythological or emotional vampires, but I did see things that would make a grown man question the world he lived in.

There was one couple who would cut each other's shoulders and then slurp the blood off in an attempt to prove themselves of the other world, denying it was self-harm at all.

It was not an uncommon sight to see a pretty girl cut her arm and then offer it out to any guy who would lean in and taste her. And people did this in full view of everyone. That's how common it had become.

The sultry allure of blood seeping from a fresh slice was all too much for those on the side lines.

They would latch on with their mouths closed and eyes glazing, revelling in the partaking of the blood streams.

But we didn't speak about mental health in the nineties. The truth is that we can't go back in time. We can't edit real life. But we can learn from the past and we can look at the reasons why.

Introduction to Vampires: Monsters of true crime.

If you're looking for fictional horror stories, this is not that book. Contained within these blackened pages are real-life tales of vampire killers, blood drinkers, criminals with a taste for blood, and those who wander the shadows of our world.

This book isn't concerned with myth or vampire lore, instead focusing on real people with vampiric tendencies. Real killers who drank the blood of their victims. Real people. Real lives.

We traverse the annals of vampiric history from the 16th Century to the 21st, beholden to no one and with no agenda in mind. When I first began writing this book and compiling the entries, I was unaware, despite what I had seen with my own eyes, of the existence of vampires.

Having completed the book at the beginning of 2023, I have come to believe that vampires do walk the earth. They don't all have capes and bad makeup and they don't hide in the darkness. They walk among us and look just like you and me.

They are our neighbours, friends, colleagues, that person sitting opposite you on the train, a family member from yesteryear. They are here and they are as real as the person you see looking back in the mirror.

The series is called Monsters of True Crime and vampires are very much considered monsters. Human creations, besotted with violence, murder, and the drinking of human blood.

At the heart of the stories are the victims, the lost souls, those who fell under the knife of a true monster. To tell the story of the vampires, is to tell their story alongside it, so that they may never be forgotten.

Here, we look at 15 real-life vampire cases from the world of true crime. In an attempt to not only understand why they committed the acts they did, but to witness the horrors of their deeds.

Did you throw the book in the bin? Or would you like to proceed?

The 15 stories contained within:

1. Drained of Blood on Walpurgis Night

During annual carnival celebrations, a call-girl was murdered in her apartment and the blood drained from her body, leading to the case being cited as proof of vampires.

2. Countess Dracula

Queen of the Vampires, castles, baths of blood, hundreds of victims, brutal slayings, legend, myth, and the worst female murderer in human history, welcome to the world of Elizabeth Bathory.

3. Soul Eater and the Runaway Devil

A man claiming to be a 300-year-old vampire, and a 12-year-old girl, fell into a forbidden love which left the girl's entire family murdered – a dark tale that concludes with a disturbing twist.

4. The Vampire Clan Murders

A group of teens obsessed with vampirism formed a cult called the Vampire Clan. Led by a disturbed man believing himself to be a 500-year-old vampire, they ended up committing cold-blooded murder.

5. The Nuremberg Vampire

A deaf and mute occultist, believing necrophilia could make him handsome, killed three people and drank their blood, before he was caught kissing a corpse in a graveyard.

6. Vampire of Anglesey

A teenager obsessed with vampire mythology, slaughtered an elderly woman, before cutting out her heart and drinking her blood.

7. Vampire of Sacramento

Richard Chase was the poster boy for bizarre serial killers whose tale included Nazi UFOs, necrophilia, cannibalism, drinking blood, and the belief he was turning to powder!

8. The Brazilian Blood-Drinker

Marcelo Costa de Andrade, the Vampire of Niterói, killed at least 14 young boys before drinking their blood to maintain his youthful appearance.

9. Vampire Killer Couple

When a German Satanist found his Princess of Darkness, they embarked on a journey through Vampirism, which ended in the murder of their friend, as a sacrifice to Satan.

10. Vampire of Hanover

A German butcher was praised for his cheap meat prices, until it was discovered he had been killing young boys by biting into their necks and drinking their blood, before selling their flesh to unsuspecting customers.

11. Marshfield Vampire Killer

A man believing he was a 700-year-old vampire shot dead his grandmother with gold bullets and drank her blood, claiming he needed the blood of his elders to survive.

12. Kiss of the Vampire

A Vampiric serial killer named Béla Kiss drained the blood of 24 victims and pickled their bodies in metal drums – before escaping capture and falling into the realm of mythology.

13. The Scottish Vampire

A Scottish man obsessed with the occult, sacrificed his friend, ate parts of head and drank his blood from a cup, in an effort to become a vampire and gain immortality.

14. The Lesbian Vampire Killer

A lesbian lover of all things occult claimed to survive off the blood of animals before convincing her friends she was a vampire who needed to kill to satisfy her craving for the red stuff.

15. The Vampire Rapist

A serial killer and government contractor, claiming to be a vampire, was exposed when a victim escaped his home – where she had been raped and drained of blood.

"I'm an energy vampire.

I JUST SUCK OFF EVERYBODY'S ENERGY,

BUT I GIVE IT BACK."

- Dolly Parton

DRAINED OF BLOOD ON WALPURGIS NIGHT

During annual carnival celebrations, a call-girl was murdered in her apartment and the blood drained from her body, leading to the case being cited as proof of vampires.

For many people, the concept of vampires are very much fictional monsters, brought to life by fantastical authors and historical inaccuracies. For others, vampires are as real as the person sitting next to you on the bus – at night.

Some killers who have been attributed the title of vampire were known to have sipped the blood of their victims or eaten part of their remains. The line between vampirism and cannibalism is drawn at consumption of the flesh, where flesh is eaten only to consume the blood.

Some killers were known to have something called clinical vampirism, referred to as Renfield Syndrome. It is a rare psychiatric disorder in which the sufferer feels a compulsion to consume blood by drinking or eating organs. The disorder is classified as some rare types of schizophrenia or paraphilia.

Some people live a vampiric lifestyle, preferring to practice safe blood-drawing techniques from close partners or donors. They do this because they believe the blood keeps them strong or they have a blood fetish.

The fictional vampire is harder to prove. However, there is one bizarre murder case that has never been solved and is still cited today as the Atlas Vampire case. It begins with a prostitute in 1930s Sweden.

Atlas

On 30th April 1932, the residents of Stockholm were celebrating Walpurgis Night, which is a traditional holiday celebrated annually in Northern Europe and Scandinavia. In Sweden, typical holiday activities include the singing of traditional spring folk songs and the lighting of bonfires. It is an event and party which continues long into the weekend.

In the Stockholm region of Atlas near Sankt Eriksplan, 32-year-old sex worker Lilly Lindeström paid her rent to the landlord then went back to her apartment to meet a client. The apartment block was a known to be home to several prostitutes, including Lilly's friend, 35-year-old Minnie Jansson.

Later that evening, as the celebrations were continuing outside, Lilly knocked on Minnie's door to borrow a condom, which was a usual thing to do in the block. Minnie sometimes worked as a prostitute and helped look out for girls in the area.

A little while later, at 9pm, a dishevelled Lilly knocked on the door again, wearing only a coat covering her nude body, and asked for another condom as the first one had broken. It was the last time that Lilly was seen alive.

Minnie went to check on her friend the following morning but Lilly didn't answer the door. Minnie assumed that Lilly was continuing the Walpurgis Night celebrations. It was four days later on 4th May when Minnie decided to call the police after becoming concerned she hadn't heard from her friend.

Discovery

Police turned up at Lilly's apartment to perform a welfare check. Upon entering the apartment they were met with a horrific sight. Lilly had been dead for three days and was found nude lying face down on an ottoman.

Her head was rested on her left arm and it appeared she had been positioned as such. Blood had dripped to the floor from a large wound on the right side of her head. It seemed she had died from being beaten to death with a hard object.

There was a used condom left in her anus, supposedly from the last client she had been with. Her clothes were folded neatly on a chair next to the ottoman, and the apartment was clean and untouched.

If the sight of the stiff nude corpse was shocking enough, there was something else wrong with the body. Due to the suspicious nature of the death, a physician was called in to perform an autopsy. He revealed that almost all of Lilly's blood had been drained.

A bloodstained soup ladle in the sink suggested the killer had drunk some of the blood at the scene. This combined with traces of saliva on Lilly's neck and body led to the conclusion that someone had consumed her blood. When the media got hold of the story, the Atlas Vampire was born.

Blood drinking

The physician claimed the head wounds were probably caused by a small section of lead pipe, and that Lilly had been struck from behind. Though some of the blood was consumed at the scene, it was suggested more blood may have been taken away in small containers.

It was later suspected the lack of blood may have been to do with the massive wound on her head, but the bloodstained ladle in the sink – which wouldn't have been heavy enough to kill her – suggested otherwise.

Many reports claim that all her blood had been drained but it simply wasn't the case, at least not according to official reports of the day. The fact remained that Lilly had been brutally murdered and a large portion of blood had exited her body.

One of the investigators, Alvar Zetterquist, wrote about the case later in his life and said the killer had left no evidence behind. There were no fingerprints, no hairs, no used drinking glass, no cigarettes, nothing to connect anyone with the crime.

The police searched Lilly's apartment inch by inch and found no clues. They also interviewed everyone living in the building and searched the area around it but had nothing to go on.

The murder weapon was never found. It was believed the killer visited Lilly with the weapon and took it with him when he left. It is suspected he was the client that Lilly had to get a second condom for.

In 1930s Sweden, sex workers were generally picked up on the street. Lilly was an oddity at the time in that she allowed clients to visit her at her apartment, foreshadowing the move from street prostitution to in-house call-girls and escorts.

Because of her unique work method, she may have attracted clientele that preferred to be more discreet in the way they carried out their business.

Mystery

Due to the lack of evidence, the case went cold quickly and it became a footnote in the history of 1930s Sweden. Yet, as the decades went by, the case was cited as one of the most infamous cases of real-life vampire attacks in history.

Was a vampire really responsible for the murder of Lily Lindeström? Well, that depends on how much you want to believe in vampires or in the monstrous capabilities of humans themselves. There was a lot of blood missing from Lilly's body but a lot of that was to do with the massive wound on her head.

We do know that throughout history there have been cases of clinical vampirism, as in the crimes of Kurten and Chase. It then remains plausible that whoever murdered Lilly was a killer who had a desire or need to drink another human's blood, indicating the killer would have killed again.

Yet, there is no other case like it in Sweden during that time.

What is mysterious is that police found no clues aside from the saliva on Lilly's neck and body. Due to the murder taking place in the pre-DNA era, there is no way to test the evidence today, despite claims it is being held at the Swedish Police Museum.

Perhaps Lilly had been killed by a foreigner visiting Stockholm for the Walpurgis Night celebrations or maybe a local who had already planned to kill her. Her schedule would have been easy to uncover and she would have been easily contactable.

Due to the lack of evidence, one theory points to a police officer, who would have known how to clean the scene and leave no trace he was ever there. Could the lack of evidence itself have been – evidence?

Another theory points to a madman using the spaces between the walls of the apartment block to spy on call-girls. After being caught by Lilly, he was forced to kill her and redress the crime scene before making his way back into the walls.

Perhaps, just perhaps, there may have been a mythical creature involved – but then, what kind of vampire uses condoms? Despite the enticing story of the Atlas Vampire, what remains certain is that Lilly Lindeström was brutally killed in her apartment and the case has never been solved.

"Vampires found a loophole
IN THE ONE THING WE CAN
NEVER ESCAPE: DEATH."

COUNTESS DRACULA

Queen of the Vampires, castles, baths of blood, hundreds of victims, brutal slayings, legend, myth, and the worst female murderer in human history, welcome to the world of Elizabeth Bathory.

The name of Bathory invokes images of a woman bathing in the blood of virgins, which would be horrific enough even in the realm of horror movies, where the legend has perpetuated. Unsettling then that the truth is even worse than the mind can endure.

When tales of her evil escaped her domain, she was ultimately not even sent to trial, instead being locked up in a windowless room in her castle, to rot until her eventual death in 1614, when she was 54-years-old.

Her legend in the realm of vampirism is second only to that of Count Dracula himself. Born in

1560 to the wealthy Bathory family, in Transylvania, Hungary. They ruled Transylvania as if it were an independent principality, such was the power they wielded.

Though Transylvania is now part of Romania, from the year 1003 to 1918, the region was part of historical Hungary, until the Austria-Hungary alliance was destroyed in the First World War, leading to the Union of Romania.

Witness accounts of the time suggested the Blood Countess may have killed up to 650 people, with the very lowest figure given as 80, of which she was charged. So what happened to the once innocent Elizabeth that led to her killing up to 650 people?

Inbreeding and blood medicine

In her formative years, up until the age of 10, Elizabeth was known to have suffered from multiple seizures which modern-day research suggests would have been the consequence of epilepsy.

It is claimed in some circles, that her parents were actually related and had given birth to Elizabeth through their inbreeding. Inbreeding has been common among humans for at least 2,000 years, predominantly in Northern Africa, rural Europe, and the Middle East.

In the 16th Century, when Elizabeth was a child, the cure for conditions similar to the seizures of epilepsy were how to put this – bizarre. The blood of a seemingly healthy person was applied to the lips of the sufferer. After the seizure ended, the sufferer would be fed a mix of healthy blood and grounded-up human skull.

All of this when Elizabeth was a mere child. It's not too big of a stretch to suggest using the blood of others would have been a way to make her feel better, a possible reason why she killed. It also would have had a psychological impact far greater that many at the time would have realised.

She was also witness to the severe beatings of servants and was once known to laugh out loud at the punishment of a servant whose crime had been stealing. It was said that the man's punishment was to be sewn into the body of a horse.

And yet, it wasn't the worst thing that Elizabeth would experience in her childhood.

Child marriage and baby killings

When Elizabeth was 10-years-old, she was engaged to a member of another wealthy and aristocratic Hungarian family, a 15-year-old Count named Ferenc Nádasdy. In that time period, many proposed marriages of this sort were mostly political arrangements between rich families.

At the age of 13, Elizabeth became pregnant by a lover who was not part of the aristocratic circles, a peasant boy from the local villages. She gave birth to a baby boy and apparently gave the child away in secrecy. When Nádasdy found out, he tracked down the family and ordered the baby be castrated and torn apart by dogs.

On 8th May 1575, when she was 15, Elizabeth married Nádasdy at a ceremony said to have been host to over 4,000 guests. As Elizabeth's family was of a higher social standing, she refused to change her last name, and her new husband took the name of Bathory.

Elizabeth had been sexually active since the age of 10 and was known to have taken secret lovers in her family's castle when Nádasdy was away. Because Nádasdy was a soldier, and an ambitious one at that, he was often away on war campaigns and other military actions.

The young couple split their time between Castle Sárvár and the Castle of Csejte, with Csejte now being located in modern-day Slovakia. Elizabeth was trained on how to run the estates in her husband's absence.

Elizabeth's wedding gift was the Castle of Csejte, set against the Carpathian mountains. This included the large country house and 17 local villages – something that may have proved vital to her getting away with so many murders.

Advantage of position

In 1578, when Elizabeth was 18, her husband, then 23, led the Hungarian troops to war and would continue to fight against the Ottoman empire up until his death in 1604. This meant that Elizabeth was left mostly alone to run his business affairs and the estates of both their families.

After her husband left for war, Elizabeth took many lovers, mostly from the villages, to satisfy her intense sexual desires. She ended up having at least four children with her husband, though some claim they were illegitimate offspring. Regardless, they were looked after by the same Governess who had looked after Elizabeth, who had little to do with her own children's lives.

Nádasdy died in 1604 after damage to his legs suffered in war. But unknown to Nádasdy, Elizabeth had already been killing, it wasn't until his death that the murders and stories of torture escalated rapidly.

By 1602, whispers around the villages were already being spread of something untoward happening at the Castle of Csejte. Servants were going missing and Elizabeth was hiring new servants on a regular basis with no details of what had happened to the previous ones.

Initially, many people were not too concerned, as unfortunately in the 16th and 17th Centuries, peasants were seen as disposable, and their lives expendable. Any questions brought to Elizabeth were dispelled easily enough on account of her wealth and familial position.

A position that would allow her to torture, maim, and kill without consequence.

The horror

Shortly after Nádasdy's death, and due to the rumours that had been circulating, a Lutheran minister named István Magyari suggested Elizabeth had been committing atrocities, but it took another six years for them to be taken seriously.

In 1610, King Matthias II assigned György Thurzó, the Palatine of Hungary (an official feudal investigator), to investigate the stories that were coming out of Bathory's domain. What Thurzó heard while building a case would horrify him and others until the end of their days.

At first, Elizabeth was accused of killing her servants but later of killing young girls who had been sent to her castle by unsuspecting family members, to learn good manners. It was suggested to Thurzó that Elizabeth believed drinking the blood of young girls would preserve her youthfulness and looks.

Witnesses inside the castle said that Elizabeth would use scissors to stab and bite their breasts, faces, hands, and legs. She would stick hot needles into their lips, under their fingernails, and burn them with hot metal items such as coins and keys. Others she would beat with clubs and let them starve to death.

Other tortures included pouring ice water over the naked bodies and leaving them in the courtyard to freeze to death. She would cover some in honey to be eaten by ants and insects, along with sewing their lips together, and biting off chunks of flesh from their faces.

One of her more popular tortures was to use her beloved scissors to slice open the skin between her victim's fingers. But as the witness accounts went on, the stories became more unreal and absurd.

Some witnesses accused her of cannibalism and blood drinking and others claimed they had seen her have sex with the devil himself. She was accused of Satanism, witchcraft, and practising black magic. Ultimately, she bathed in the blood of her victims.

House arrest

By 1611, Thurzó had recorded over 300 witness statements of varying degrees from servants, villagers, and people known to Elizabeth. He laid charges at her feet, accusing her of killing – or being associated with the death of – 80 girls. When he arrived at the castle, he recorded seeing the dead body of a young girl, and a living girl being used as '*prey*' within the castle walls.

One witness, who claimed to have close ties with Elizabeth and assisted her with '*collecting*' the girls, said that Elizabeth had a diary which detailed the names of her victims. It was said the book, which is now conveniently lost to time, listed the names of 650 victims.

One of Elizabeth's more trusted servants who worked in the care of her children, was later convicted of witchcraft and burned alive at the stake. It was unknown if it was she who bore witness to the book of victims.

The Budapest City Archives, which holds records of the accusations against Elizabeth Bathory, shows that most of the victims were between the ages of 10 to 14, and were commonly burned with hot tongs before being thrown in cold water.

The archived witness statements claim the dead were buried in graveyards around the castle and villages, almost all in unmarked graves. There were even suggestions some of the dead had been buried in the castle itself or burned to ashes.

Due to the Bathory name holding such weight in Hungary at the time, it was believed that a trial and execution would have caused a public scandal. Elizabeth's adult children, and other influential families, claimed the entire hierarchy would be disgraced if she were to be executed.

The initial plan was to make her disappear and embed her with a nunnery in the North of the country but rumours of murderous nobility had taken hold of Hungary, and rebellion was in the air. It was decided that Elizabeth should be placed under house arrest for the rest of her life.

There is a perpetuating legend that Elizabeth was locked into a single windowless room until her death in 1614, but it has recently been suggested she was allowed free movement within the walls of the castle.

Castle arrest, it seemed, would be a better choice of words.

The 'Bathory was a victim' conspiracy

There is one side to Elizabeth's story and legend that is rarely spoken about. That Elizabeth Bathory was no more than a pawn in a game of power to gain a foothold in the Carpathians, and more importantly the strategic position of the Castle of Csejte.

Before Bathory's family and other families intervened, the King wished her executed because it meant he could seize her land – and castle. To have her executed, he needed a story so grim and nasty that execution would be the only desired outcome.

Research shows that many witnesses accounts were based on hearsay, in that they had no first-hand evidence of the tortures and deaths ever taking place. Most servants confessed only under torture by the Hungarian Kingdom, and there exists no document prior to Thurzó's arrival that anyone had complained about Elizabeth at all, which would have been unusual for the time period.

Upon the death of her husband, Elizabeth owned strategically important land, with the castle and villages alone worth an extraordinary amount of wealth. Her wealth and stronghold may have scared the King and he sought to discredit her life before claiming it for himself. It would have been the only way to do it, without enraging the powerful wealthy families in his kingdom.

There is also a suggestion that Elizabeth's husband had been in a huge amount of debt and that Elizabeth refused to sell any of her wealth to settle it, so the Kingdom sought other ways to be rid of her.

The story of Elizabeth Bathory is embedded into popular culture, mystery stories, and true crime tales. But the question remains; was Elizabeth the torturous blood-bathing murderess she has always been made out to be, or someone who was in the way of an ambitious kingdom?

Yet, it is still said the blood of her victims is ingrained into the walls of the Castle of Csejte itself, which can be visited today. Elizabeth was ultimately buried at the Bathory family crypt. When the crypt was opened in 1995 – Elizabeth's body was nowhere to be seen.

"Even if people don't believe in THE EXISTENCE OF VAMPIRES, THEY ARE SUCKED INTO THE POSSIBILITY."

SOUL EATER AND THE RUNAWAY DEVIL

A man claiming to be a 300-year-old vampire, and a 12-year-old girl, fell into a forbidden love which left the girl's entire family murdered – a dark tale that concludes with a disturbing twist.

There is nothing more disturbing than a child who commits pre-meditated murder, except perhaps a child who commits murder with an adult boyfriend who believed he was a vampire.

In Medicine Hat, Alberta, Canada, on 23rd April 2006, 12-year-old Jasmine Richardson and her 23-year-old boyfriend Jeremy Steinke killed three members of Jasmine's family. They had spent many weeks planning the murders in revenge for Jasmine's parents disapproving of their relationship.

Jasmine looked older for her age and was known to go out with friends to rock concerts, and it was there she allegedly met the 23-year-old Jeremy, just three months before the murders. Jasmine set up user profiles on the Vampire Freaks forum, and a Canadian forum and messaging board called Nexopia.

On both sites she listed her age as 15 and used it as a way to converse with Jeremy, and their relationship grew to the point where Jasmine became besotted with the idea of murder, propagated by a love of blood and a fascination with human anatomy. She went under the username of Runaway Devil, while Jeremy used Soul Eater, among others.

Jeremy too had some unusual preferences. He was known to enjoy the taste of blood and carried around a small vial of his own blood around his neck for whenever the hunger struck. He told his friends that he was a 300-year-old vampire, lost in time, just trying to survive in the new world.

Natural Born Killers

When Jasmine's parents found out about the burgeoning relationship, they tried to stop Jasmine seeing Jeremy, but it didn't end well. That fascination with blood, led Jasmine to believe her parents needed to die as punishment for telling her what to do and trying to end her relationship.

Jeremy was fascinated with the Oliver Stone movie Natural Born Killers, about a young couple who kill the lead female's parents then go on a killing spree. He believed that he and his new young girlfriend should use the film as a starting point for their life together.

They planned the murder of Jasmine's family and thought of it as the right thing to do, to rid themselves of imposing mortals who would do nothing to stop their forbidden love.

In some of her messages to Jeremy, Jasmine shared photographs of herself holding a gun and posing in gothic makeup. The love between them was seemingly growing stronger in her heart. Just hours before the murders, she posted; *welcome to my tragic end*.

The same morning, at his trailer, Jeremy watched Natural Born Killers again. He told his friends that he and Jasmine should go about their plans for murder in the same way. He also claimed the film to be the greatest love story of all time.

Bloodstained house

On the morning of the 23rd, Jeremy and Jasmine met up, went to her parents' house and stabbed to death her father, 42-year-old Marc Richardson, her mother, 48-year-old Debra, and Jasmine's brother, eight-year-old Tyler.

Police arrived shortly after when a friend of the family discovered the bodies inside the bloodstained house. The parents were found in the basement, stabbed to death, and Tyler was found on the first floor of the property with his throat cut.

Jasmine was thought to be missing, and as such she was suspected to have been kidnapped and killed elsewhere. When police began searching for her, they came across the messages between her and Jeremy, and shockingly realised she had been involved in the murders.

The following day, the pair were arrested in Leader, Saskatchewan, approximately 80 miles south of the Richardson house. Steinke had enlisted the help of friend and drug addict, 19-year-old Kacy Lancaster, to drive them away in her pick-up truck – along with three underage friends.

Lancaster was later charged as being an accessory to murder but the charges were dropped for the focus to remain on Jeremy and Jasmine. Shortly after the arrests, Jeremy asked Jasmine to marry him, and still besotted with her 300-year-old vampire, she agreed.

Punishments

While claiming to be innocent, Jeremy fell into the trap of confessing to an undercover police officer placed in his cell, where he told the officer he had killed the parents. He was ultimately found guilty on three counts of first-degree murder in 2008, and sentenced to three life sentences, one for each of the victims.

Jasmine's trial was a little trickier. At the time, her name could not be published due to limitations in the Youth Criminal Justice Act. In Canada, any person under the age of 14 at the time of a crime cannot be sentenced as an adult.

In July 2007, a whole year before Jeremy was convicted, the then 13-year-old Jasmine was found guilty of three counts of first-degree murder, the youngest person in Canada to be convicted of multiple first-degree murders. She was sentenced to the maximum allowable term of ten years in a psychiatric institution.

In the Autumn of 2011, Jasmine was released from the institution and spent the next four-and-a half-years under a community rehabilitation order. On 6th May 2016, aged 22, Jasmine was released of any further court orders and conditions, and freed to live her life.

But let's step back for a moment, because there is more to this case than meets the eye and you were promised a twist in the blurb. It doesn't matter how readers or researchers look at the case, it is horrific and disturbing. Yet, the deeper we dig into the Richardson case, the more disturbing it could actually be.

As crazy as he was

Newspaper reports at the time and court documents reveal that something else may have been going on with the pair. It's easy to forget that a 12-year-old girl – a child – was involved in these killings, however we have to look at where we draw the line of innocence. It's also important to remember that Jasmine was found guilty of committing three pre-meditated murders.

As they fled Medicine Hat, one of the underage children in the pick-up truck, testified that a newspaper report of the murders brought smiles to the faces of the killers, and they jested over the fact the paper had used Jasmine's old school photograph.

On the morning of the murders, when Jeremy was watching Natural Born Killers, his friends testified about a phone call they overheard. They claimed he was on the phone in the kitchen pacing back and forth, panicking about something they couldn't understand at the time.

He was heard saying, '*I don't want to do this. Are you sure you want to do this*?' The same witness claimed that Jasmine was the one who begged Jeremy to do it – for her.

Returning to watch the film, he sat down during a scene where the lead female, played by Juliette Lewis, spares her younger brother. Jeremy pointed at the screen and said, '*that's where we would do it different. She (Jasmine) would kill her brother.*'

Many of the friends claimed he spoke about killing Jasmine's parents as she wouldn't be strong enough to kill the adults, but she could kill her brother. The friends tried to talk him out of it but were unsure if he would go through with any of it, or if he was even being genuine.

He told his friends they wouldn't understand, and in Jasmine, he had found someone as crazy as he was. In some ways, he was right.

Manipulative sociopath

Jasmine was convicted of first-degree murder a year before Jeremy based on the testimony of some of the people who later testified at Jeremy's trial. Even after the story had come out, it was insinuated by the press that Jeremy alone had killed all three victims.

According to Jeremy and some of the witnesses, it was Jasmine who had masterminded the plan for the murders. Jasmine was known to be manipulative, cold, and sociopathic, but couldn't be described as such because her brain was considered to still be developing.

In fact, at Jasmine's trial, she admitted to killing her younger brother while he begged for his life. Tyler pleaded with her that he was '*too young to die*' but Jasmine slit his throat and watched his blood splatter the bedsheets.

Jeremy claimed that when she slit her brother's throat, '*it didn't bother her at all, she didn't cry or anything. In fact, the next day when we were on the road, she was laughing about it. She's got a few screws loose, too.*'

Could a 12-year-old girl have been so numbed by death that she manipulated a 23-year-old man into killing her family? It's possible but both of them had long been on a dark road.

Descent

Jeremy lived on a trailer park with his mother, and she said Jeremy was abused and beaten by her husband, his father, when he was younger. He had been on anti-depressants for over a decade, was a high-school dropout, and was known to be younger than his age with a sense of gullibility about him.

Even so, he stabbed Debra Richardson 12 times and left her at the bottom of the basement staircase before stabbing Marc 24 times. Their blood covered the walls as he followed his girlfriend up the stairs to her brother's room.

Even in the few months he had been with Jasmine, he dreamed of marrying her in a Gothic wedding ceremony and moving to a castle in Germany, where they could live out their dark fantasies in any way they pleased.

Growing up, Jasmine was a happy, intelligent girl until the age of 11, when she descended into an obsession with violence, became sexually active, and found solace in the world of the mythical vampire, besotted with blood.

On her profile pages of the forums, her interests were blood, darkness, human anatomy, serial killers, hatchets, criminal psychology, and '*kinky shit*'. Her heroes were Jeffrey Dahmer, Marilyn Manson, and Dani Filth from UK-based metal group, Cradle of Filth; her favourite band.

She refused to wear school uniforms and instead went around wearing short skirts, heavy black makeup, and told people she was 15 or 16, depending on what she thought she could get away with.

Lust for blood

Vampiric tendency is something occasionally noted in psychology under some cases of schizophrenia and linked to Renfield Syndrome. A patient generally displays a strong desire for blood and believes they are consuming the lifeforce of others or replenishing their own.

It is questionable why Jeremy's lawyer didn't base his defence on insanity, as Jeremy clearly had mental issues in the past, evident from the medication. He was also clearly displaying some signs of a psychological disorder, evident by his blood consumption.

Many find it disturbing that a 12-year-old girl would become so consumed by her own lust for blood, that she used a 23-year-old man to kill her parents because she wasn't strong enough, and even more worrying that she is now free to walk among us unsupervised.

Jasmine had grown up too fast, consumed by the darkness she surrounded herself with, believing it to be the best life for her. Unable to decipher art from reality, she fell into a dark web of blood lust and forbidden love.

Jeremy had long been seeking the missing half of his own dark soul, and when he found Jasmine, regardless of her age, he connected on a level beyond lust and passion, and found the person he was happy to call crazier than he was.

Together, they carved a path through the annals of true crime history that has since been unmatched in its depravity and shamefulness, underpinned by a somewhat depressing tale of two lovers under the darkness of the full moon.

'My biggest fear is that she hasn't been rehabilitated, that she's tricked those in the system, that she hasn't moved forward.' – Brent Secondiak, the first police officer to arrive at the Richardson home.

"A Vampire, like
A LADY, NEVER
REVEALS ITS TRUE AGE."

THE VAMPIRE CLAN MURDERS

A group of teens obsessed with vampirism formed a cult called the Vampire Clan. Led by a disturbed man believing himself to be a 500-year-old vampire, they ended up committing cold-blooded murder.

Reading about vampire cults and murders involving people claiming to be real vampires is like something out of a horror novel. Except, in 1996, in Florida, a cult called the Vampire Clan took part in the double slaying of an innocent couple.

The ring-leader was 16-year-old Rod Ferrell who had become obsessed with a role-playing game called Vampire: The Masquerade. The game is set in a fictional gothic-punk world where players assume the role of vampires and deal with their nightly struggles.

Involving himself deeply in the game, Ferrell, who lived in Kentucky, began to believe in his character and assumed the identity of a 500-year-old vampire named Vesago. Three of his friends, Howard Scott Anderson, 16, Charity Keesee, 16, and Dana Cooper, 19, created the cult, each having their own vampiric beliefs.

Together they practiced blood-letting, drinking each other's blood, and rituals considered to be vampiric in nature, based on some elements of the game. Ferrell began to believe he really was some form of reincarnated demon and became the de-facto leader of the cult.

On 25th November 1996, the self-named Vampire Clan, under the leadership of Ferrell invaded the home of 54-year-old Naomi Ruth Queen and 49-year-old Richard Wendorf and brutally murdered them, in an act so horrific, it brought back memories of the Manson Family Murders.

Slaughterhouse

In the city of Eustis, Florida, 17-year-old Jennifer Wendorf went home after a night out, missing her 10pm curfew, expecting her father Richard and stepmom Naomi to be mad with her. Hoping they would be asleep, she opened the front door and crept inside.

She saw Richard on the couch and breathed a sigh of relief, thinking she had successfully snuck in. When she reached the kitchen, she stepped back in horror. The cupboards and floor were covered in blood splatter, and beside the sink was Naomi's body.

Jennifer had stumbled upon a double murder so horrific, that when police arrived, they too were taken aback at the brutality of the scene. Jennifer then realised her sister Heather was missing, and so began an investigation that went to the darkest of places.

Heather was very different from Jennifer, who was a high-school cheerleader and had already received a scholarship for college. Heather, who was 15 at the time of the murders, was known to have involved herself in alternative fashions with a fascination for the occult.

The previous year, she had been out with friends in Eustis when she met Ferrell, who was enrolled at the Eustis High School. He immediately became besotted with her and concluded that Heather possessed non-human qualities such as himself.

Ferrell would walk around her neighbourhood with samurai swords and had conversations with her where he claimed to have killed his neighbour's cat and retold stories of 15th Century Paris.

Heather realised that Ferrell's vampiric lifestyle was one she had been looking for all her young life.

Without warning, Ferrell left school and returned to Kentucky. They kept in contact by phone, and Heather told him that she was unhappy with her parents as they didn't understand her. Ferrell took it to mean that she was being abused and told her to run away and be with him in Kentucky.

Vampire Hotel

Before Ferrell went to school in Florida, and around the same time he discovered the vampire role-playing game, a friend of his, Jaden Murphy, introduced him to bloodletting. Jaden claimed that vampirism reflected his soul and gave him power through the consumption of human blood.

Jaden took Ferrell to a local cemetery where they drew each other's blood to drink, claiming that giving blood as a gift was one of the greatest gifts you can give someone. When Ferrell thought about forming a cult, Jaden decided to distance himself, but had already instilled a vampiric tendency within Ferrell.

Though Ferrell is often seen as the cult's leader, it was in fact Dana Cooper who first gave the idea of the group. Cooper, who was the oldest of the group, at 19, led Ferrell to an abandoned home that she called the Vampire Hotel.

The derelict property in the middle of the woods around Kentucky Lake, was secluded enough to remain hidden from nearby paths. It was there where the group was formed, and where they would torture one another for consumption of blood and for sexual gratification.

Soon after the Vampire Clan had been formed, Heather was convinced to write a goodbye letter to her parents and end the relationship with her boyfriend, Jeremy Hueber. The four members of the Vampire Clan planned to travel to Florida, pick her up and take her away from the hell of her home life.

Jeremy later said he had already split up with Heather due to her bizarre fantasies and her claim that Ferrell was a higher power that she had to obey. She believed him to be the 500-year-old vampire he had claimed and was going to run away with the Vampire Clan.

The group drove 800 miles from Kentucky to Eustis in Anderson's car and met Heather down the road from her parents' house. When the car got a flat tyre shortly after, Ferrell and Anderson decided to steal the Wendorf's vehicle.

Though Ferrell claimed the initial intention was to steal the car, it became clear he wanted Heather's parents to suffer for the supposed hell they had put their daughter through. He and Anderson walked past the parked Wendorf car and into the property through the unlocked garage.

'V'

Richard Wendorf was asleep on the couch and Naomi was in the shower. Ferrell had picked up a crowbar from the garage and when he saw Richard laying down, he battered him to death, fracturing his skull and breaking multiple bones, killing him instantly.

Unaware of the home invasion and attack, Naomi exited the shower and found Ferrell and Anderson standing over her partner's bloodied body. Ferrell grabbed the crowbar and chased her into the kitchen where he bashed her over the head multiple times.

He later claimed he was going to let her live but she had attacked him first. After killing Naomi, Ferrell returned to Richard's body and burned the letter 'V' into his upper chest, later confirming it to be the symbol for the Vampire Clan, and his calling card.

They took Richard's vehicle and met up with Heather, Keesee, and Cooper, further down the road. By all accounts, Heather wasn't told of her parent's death until much later. Out of ear's reach, Ferrell described the murders in detail to Keesee and Cooper.

For the next four days, police tracked the Vampire Clan across four different states until they were finally arrested in Baton Rouge, Louisiana. The group had visited Keesee's mother who gave them some money then immediately informed the police of their whereabouts after seeing the story of the murders on the news. She helped lure them to a hotel where a police ambush was waiting.

Creatures of the night

The group were held at a local jail before being extradited to Florida. The case made national headlines and many photos found their way to the newspapers, including one of Ferrell hanging upside down by his feet, with his arms crossed over his chest, as if he were a sleeping vampire bat.

In February 1998, Ferrell pleaded guilty to the murders of Richard and Naomi and was sentenced to death, becoming the youngest person in Florida to be on death row, despite his lawyers claiming insanity. He was later diagnosed with various personality disorders.

Due to later changes in the law, his sentence was commuted to life in prison without the possibility of parole. Ferrell claimed that everyone else in the Vampire Clan, including Heather, were innocent, except Anderson who was simply an accessory and bystander to the murders.

Anderson was also convicted of the murders under 'felony murder' law and sentenced to life in prison. Such laws allow for people to be convicted of murder if a death occurs because of a crime they commit, even if they were not the direct killer. Anderson broke into the house with Ferrell and was considered complicit in the murders.

Charity Keesee and Dana Cooper were convicted of two counts of third-degree murder and sentenced to 10 years and 17 years respectively. Keesee was released eight year later in 2006, and Cooper 13 years later in October 2011.

The four members of the Vampire Clan said that Heather didn't know Ferrell was going to kill her parents, and only found out when they were arrested. Bizarrely, two witnesses claiming to be friends of Heather came forward to say that she wanted her parents dead. Both failed polygraph tests and neither were known friends of Heather, just those wanting their 15 minutes of infamy.

Heather was cleared of any wrongdoing even though she fled with the Vampire Clan, due to her not knowing about the murders. She went on to live a relatively normal life away from the influence of manipulators and cults.

Whether you believe in the mythological vampire as having a basis in reality or not, there are those as proven in this story who practice vampirism in the belief they are real-life creatures of the night. What could be more worrying, that these creatures truly exist, or that a group of teenagers fell under the spell of vampirism and killed to fit their unusual lifestyle.

"When other little girls wanted to be ballet dancers, I kind of wanted to be a vampire."

- Angelina Jolie

THE NUREMBERG VAMPIRE

A deaf and mute occultist, believing necrophilia could make him handsome, killed three people and drank their blood, before he was caught kissing a corpse in a graveyard.

I n the middle of the night in May 1972, in Nuremberg, Germany, morgue attendant George Warmuth spotted a shadowy figure in the graveyard. As he drew closer to see who it was, he recoiled in shock, as the figure was holding a corpse in his arms, locked in a passionate kiss.

George wouldn't know it at the time, but he had stumbled across a triple murderer, necrophile, grave-robber, cannibal, and blood drinker named Kuno Hoffman, known later across Germany and the world as the Vampire of Nuremberg.

Kuno was born in 1931 and raised in a violent household, where his father would abuse him constantly. On one occasion, Kuno was beaten so badly by his father, that it would cause him to lose his speech and hearing, causing him to become deaf and mute.

Needless to say, his teenage years were marred with crime and mental health issues, which had led him to spending many years in and out of psychiatric hospitals and prisons. He allegedly escaped from 12 psychiatric hospitals throughout the years.

When he was convicted of a theft charge in the early 1960s, Kuno spent nine years in prison. While there, he became obsessed with the occult and satanism, and consumed many books on the subjects, which led to a fascination with rituals involving vampirism and necrophilia.

Copulating with the dead

When he was released from prison, he continued to study books on the occult and satanism, in an effort to understand what he called the occult sciences. For many years, due to his mental health status and disabilities, Kuno had come to belief he was ugly and weak.

The entire purpose of studying the occult was to look for ways to make himself handsome and strong. Unable to hold down a job due to his condition and inability to stick it out, the occult alleviated his loneliness and offered a promise of a new life.

Kuno developed the notion that by performing satanic rituals over corpses and then drinking their blood, he would achieve his goals of becoming handsome and strong. In early 1971, Kuno turned his dreams of perfection into reality.

But to attain his dreams, he needed the perfect corpse, and there was no better corpse than someone who had recently died. He perused the local newspapers for obituaries and picked the recent dead who attracted him the most.

Under cover of night, Kuno broke into various graveyards and mortuaries to copulate with the dead. He was able to make copies of cemetery keys and used them to hide among the tombstones before digging up a corpse then stabbing and slicing the body with a razor to retrieve blood.

He would bite the corpses, drink as much of the drying blood as possible and chew the flesh. His real prize, however, were the bodies in the mortuaries, as he believed the blood to be fresher and was able to do things he couldn't always do in the graveyards – engage in necrophilia.

35 corpses

Necrophilia is one of those unsavoury human traits that we rarely hear about, and for some of us, the less we know about it, the better. For the Vampire of Nuremberg, although starting out as a means to an end, he began to enjoy the act and focused his attention on young women who had died in the region – young women he found himself sexually attracted to.

After working out which mortuary their bodies would be held at, he broke in and danced with the dead for as long as he pleased. When morticians and morgue workers turned up for work, they found their recently dead corpses had been sexually assaulted and butchered.

It was estimated that between 1971 and 1972, at least 35 corpses had been attacked in such a way, with some of them dug up in cemeteries. Almost all of the female corpses showed evidence of penetration, with some of them having been beheaded.

By early 1972, police were made aware of the unusual attacks on corpses but had no suspect in sight. Nuremberg wasn't the best of places in the early 1970s due to the fallout of the Second World War but a vampiric necrophile on the loose was certainly abnormal and warranted much attention.

But Kuno was just getting started. As much as he enjoyed consuming the blood of recently dead corpses, he found the quality of blood he drank from the bodies was not quite as good as he wanted and so his attention turned to the living.

Triple murder

On 6th May 1972, 24-year-old Markus Adler and his fiancée, 18-year-old Ruth Lissy, were sitting in their car, on a romantic night out, unaware of the danger nearby. Kuno was watching them from the shadows, gun in hand, ready to claim the freshest of corpses for their blood.

He approached from the darkness and caught the couple off-guard before shooting them dead through the window of the car. He then cut their throats and drank the blood from their lifeless bodies before having sex with Ruth's corpse.

Two days later, empowered with the rush of fresh blood, Kuno went on the prowl for another victim and found a young woman walking alone at night. He approached her from behind and shot her in the back of the head before slicing her arteries and drinking from her body.

She too was raped after death but her name has never been released in Germany, because of various privacy laws. This likely meant she was under the age of 18 at the time of her murder and caused a massive police investigation when her death was linked to the previous two.

Then, on 10th May 1972, with three linked murders in the region, and a serial killer on the loose, cemetery and mortuary workers were put on alert, which led to morgue attendant George Warmuth running a security check on the nearby cemetery.

It was there, he witnessed a man in the shadows holding a corpse in his arms and locked in a passionate embrace. A man the local media had come to call the Vampire of Nuremberg. When Kuno realised he was being watched, he dropped the body, pulled his gun and fired at Warmuth.

Cold-blooded vampirism

The bullet missed Warmuth by inches and he survived the attack but Kuno had eloped. As Kuno ran under the direct moonlight, Warmuth noted everything he could about his appearance, which would lead to Kuno's arrest in the early hours of the following morning.

Police quickly discovered that Kuno had been seen by other witnesses hanging around cemeteries and mortuaries. The witness statements, combined with Kuno's long history of stays in psychiatric hospitals, made him the prime suspect.

Upon his arrest, Kuno readily admitted to the grave robberies, blood drinking, necrophilia, and the three murders. He casually explained that when he found the corpses to be of a low-quality blood-drinking experience, he moved to claiming fresh corpses.

He also claimed he was going to continue killing and drinking blood until the ritual of handsomeness and strength had been achieved but admitted at the same time he had come to enjoy the act of blood-drinking as a fetish despite the original intent of rituals.

At his trial, it was suspected that Kuno would be able to plead not guilty on grounds of insanity but it was concluded by the court that Kuno knew the difference between right and wrong and would stand trial for triple murder, grave-robbing, satanism, and copulation with a corpse.

He was sentenced to life in prison in late 1972, where he remained until his death a few years later. Though his cause of death has never been released, it was suspected to be down to complications following consumption of raw human flesh and blood.

While in prison, he asked fellow prisoners and guards if they had access to the blood of virgins to help him live longer. His requests were obviously denied. The Vampire of Nuremberg remains one of Germany's and the world's most unusual cases of cold-blooded vampirism.

"I took mythology a lot MORE SERIOUSLY SINCE I'D BECOME A VAMPIRE."

- Stephenie Meyer

VAMPIRE OF ANGLESEY

A teenager obsessed with vampire mythology, slaughtered an elderly woman, before cutting out her heart and drinking her blood.

Anglesey is an island off the north-west coast of Wales, home to approximately 70,000 people. It's not a place one usually associated with cold-blooded murder, let alone vampires. But in 2001, a teenage student changed all that.

17-year-old Matthew Hardman was considered a remarkably normal young man who lived a remarkably normal life. His mother was a nurse and his father was a firefighter, both of whom had successful careers in their fields.

When Matthew was just a boy, his father unexpectedly died of an asthma attack, leaving his mother distraught, and Matthew struggling to comprehend the death. It has long been suspected that his love with the vampire myth developed as he sought a way to cheat death.

His teachers kept a close eye on him, unsure how much his father's death would affect him. And yet, there was seemingly nothing untoward, as he was known to have a good sense of humour, and a good academic record.

Despite struggling with writing and spelling, he was by all accounts considered a happy, healthy young man. Outside of school, he played video games, watched movies, loved all kinds of music, and went out drinking on occasion with his friends.

When he was 16, he was enrolled in an arts and design college course and became an exemplary student. But unknown to everyone around him, Matthew had developed something else along the way — a fascination with vampires and the mythology of reincarnation.

Fascination with vampires

It remains unclear where the vampire connection originated from but all the entertainment forms he consumed contained some kind of vampiric myth, albeit minor in some cases.

Films and TV of the time were full of popcorn programming, from Buffy, Blade, Dracula 2000,

Bram Stoker's Dracula, and From Dusk Till Dawn. Horror games of the time were Silent Hill, Resident Evil 3, Carrier, and Clive Barker's Undying. Nothing that would seemingly lead someone to murder.

And yet there were films throughout the 1990s, that were specifically cited as influencing murders. These included Scream and Interview with the Vampire. However, it's important to note that only those already susceptible to violence are influenced by such films.

Wherever Matthew's fascination with vampires came from, whether from his father's death or the entertainment media around him, one thing was for sure. Matthew was about to commit one of the most horrific crimes ever seen on the Welsh island.

He had come to believe that vampires were real, and as part of their existence, they drank human blood. More importantly, he believed that by drinking human blood, he would become immortal, something that would have saved his father.

During the same year as the murder, Matthew's short-term German girlfriend learned of his obsession with vampires and would later testify at his trial. He had told her that Anglesey was the perfect hunting ground for vampires, because of the aging population.

He also begged his girlfriend to bite him, believing she was a vampire of German origin. So much so, that he screamed at her when she wouldn't do it. When she refused, Matthew came up with a plan of killing an elderly resident of Anglesey.

The Devil has been to Anglesey

On the evening of 24th November 2011, in Llanfairpwll, 90-year-old widow Mabel Leyshon was sitting in her armchair, watching TV, as she did on most nights since her husband's passing. Matthew briefly worked as a paperboy and delivered newspapers to Mabel, so he knew she would be alone.

He broke into the bungalow through a rear window and crept into the living room where Mabel was sitting. Then, without a second's hesitation, he stabbed her from behind and they briefly fought before Mabel fell back into the armchair. Matthew went on to stab her 22 times.

The wound to her chest was eight inches long and nine inches wide, exposing most of her innards. He then sliced her legs and began draining blood into a small saucepan he had taken from the kitchen. Once the blood had partly filled the saucepan, he lifted it up and drank from it.

Not content with drinking her blood, he cut out her heart and removed it from her chest. Then he wrapped it in a newspaper, and placed it into the same saucepan, before displaying it on a silver platter on the table. He then placed two brass pokers at her feet in the shape of a crucifix and a red candle on the sideboard, before fleeing the home.

At lunchtime the next day, a meals-on-wheels volunteer carer went to the house to deliver Mabel her regular Sunday lunch. When they saw the rear window had been broken, the police were called, who discovered a murder so horrific, it would taint Anglesey and the town of Llanfairpwll forever.

One of the officers told hungry reporters that the crime was so horrific he believed the Devil had been to Anglesey. The manhunt to find the killer took six weeks, because despite the amount of evidence left at the scene, Matthew's DNA was not already on record, as he had never committed a crime.

As Christmas approached, the elderly residents of Anglesey were becoming more nervous as the killer had not been caught. Unknown to the residents, the police were closing in on Matthew Hardman, a teenager who seemingly wouldn't hurt a fly.

Vampire rights movement

All lines of enquiry were pointing towards Matthew and with all the evidence they needed, police went to his family home to make an arrest. There, they found all the evidence they needed. DNA evidence proved that Matthew was the killer.

He had left his own DNA and multiple fingerprints at the scene of the crime, and his lip imprint was on the saucepan he had drunk from. His girlfriend came forward to tell police of his unusual appetite for all things vampire and told them how Matthew had explained Anglesey was prime vampire hunting ground.

Inside Matthew's house, they found the knife used to slaughter Mabel, still stained in her blood. They also found a copy of Bram Stoker's Dracula and a library book titled The Devil: an autobiography. Which wasn't so bad until they found a magazine explaining how to carry out a black mass and cook human flesh.

Matthew had also visited various vampire websites, including the Vampire Rights Movement (later popularised in the HBO series True Blood) and the Vampire/Donor site, which is now more commonly known as the Black Books Directory.

During the first three days of questioning by police, Matthew showed no emotion and spoke about the murders as if he had been watching a film. The lack of emotion disturbed those who interviewed him, as everything else pointed toward him being a remarkably normal young man.

Big Mac and fries

His trial began within a couple of months and the public learned more about the fantasy that had plagued most of his teenage years. They also learned more about the plan and how he thought he was going to get away with it.

At that time, they didn't know the name of the killer, due to Matthew being only 17. But once the sentenced was passed, and due to the high-profile nature of the case, the judge lifted an order banning his identification.

His name was already known to some reporters, who had followed police to Matthew's home, but they were stopped publishing any names or photos. One reporter went to a small hill overlooking the home and saw the house covered with forensic teams and police.

Beyond the house, and across a small field, was Mabel's bungalow. Matthew had simply walked across the field in the middle of the night, killed Mabel, performed his ritual, and traipsed back home.

When Matthew was questioned by police and asked if he wanted anything, he simply replied that he wanted a Big Mac and fries. By the time of the trial, Matthew's legal team did not put forward a defence of insanity.

It meant that Matthew would be tried with the full force of the law. Due to the overwhelming evidence against him, and after a three-week trial, Matthew was found guilty of murder, and handed down a life sentence.

At the sentencing, the judge stated that the manner of the murder was difficult to comprehend. He said that Matthew's obsession with vampires, meant that he really did believe he would achieve immortality by drinking the blood of another human.

And so it remains unusual that his legal defence team didn't push for a not guilty by way of insanity plea. However, the judge agreed that there was no psychological explanation for the behaviour and that Matthew was of sound mind.

There was no life tariff imposed on Matthew, which meant he would have served the minimum of 12 years, his sentence ending in 2013. No information on his whereabouts have been released publicly, which means he has either been transferred to a psychiatric facility or been released quietly back into society under a new name, with the latter being the most likely outcome.

The judge in the trial had the final words on the case, which are a fitting end to the story of the Anglesey Vampire. 'You hoped for immortality but all you have achieved is the brutal ending of another person's life and the bringing of a life sentence upon yourself.'

"Dracula wasn't a vampire, he was a smokescreen.

A DISTRACTION, TO TAKE THE HEAT OFF THE

REAL VAMPIRES LIVING IN THE SHADOWS."

VAMPIRE OF SACRAMENTO

Richard Chase was the poster boy for bizarre serial killers whose tale included Nazi UFOs, necrophilia, cannibalism, drinking blood, and the belief he was turning to powder!

Richard Trenton Chase killed six people over a one month period from 29th December 1977 to 27th January 1978. He became known as the Vampire of Sacramento because he drank the blood of his victims, engaged in necrophilia, and ate some of their remains.

Not the nicest of chaps and we can't make excuses for him but he had a rather bizarre and upsetting childhood. Chase was born in Sacramento in 1950 and was sexually abused by his mother over the first ten years of his life.

He developed a fascination with hurting small animals, like cats and small dogs. It was this feeling of ultimate power over another's life that would eventually drive him to kill a human. He enjoyed torturing and killing small animals, and at the age of 10, Chase killed a cat he found on the street and left its body in the open.

Hurting small animals is one way a child can take out their anger and hatred. They are too small to hurt their abusers and hurt smaller animals until such time when they are big enough to hurt other humans.

During his teen years, he was able to hide his mental issues under a veil of alcohol and marijuana which was easily accessible at the time. He constantly got into trouble at school and at home because of it, but he saw it as an escape from the banalities of life and the troubles that plagued him.

The delusions set in

Chase was unable to perform sexually as he couldn't maintain an erection and this made him feel humiliated and unable to connect with other people. When he was 18, he voluntarily went to see a psychiatrist about his erection problem. It was under the counselling of his psychiatrist where he learned it was sometimes caused by the repression of anger.

After leaving his mother's house on the belief that she was trying to poison him, he rented an apartment with some friends. During his time in the apartment, it was said that Chase enjoyed walking around in the nude and was constantly high on multiple types of drugs including LSD.

During his time in the apartment he would go through many flatmates, all of which would complain to him and to the authorities about his bizarre behaviour and heavy drug use. One time he nailed the closet door shut in his bedroom because he thought that people were coming out from the darkness and invading his private space.

He began to develop severe paranoia and started to become a fully-fledged hypochondriac, believing that everything was going wrong with his body. At one point, he entered a hospital looking for the person who had stolen his pulmonary artery.

He complained that his bones were coming out through the back of his head causing his skull to split and maintained a belief that his stomach was back to front. He also claimed his heart would stop beating and then start up again after a short amount of time.

Chase would wallow in a pit of paranoid delusions and far-fetched hypochondria, brought on by child abuse and a massive consumption of drugs. When he refused to leave the apartment, his flatmates moved out instead.

His newfound isolation afforded him the possibility of acting on darker desires. He started to trap then kill more small animals. He would disembowel them and eat the raw meat. He then moved onto purchasing small pets with the intention of killing them.

Chase was under the delusion that his heart was shrinking. The consumption of raw flesh and the drinking of animal blood could stop his heart disappearing from his body altogether. He believed this to such an extent that he once injected rabbit blood directly into his veins – which didn't go to well, and he was rushed to hospital, where he got the nickname of Dracula.

Clinical Vampirism

When he was 25-years-old, he was committed as a paranoid schizophrenic to Beverly Manor Institute for the mentally insane. It is reported that anti-psychotic medicines failed to work on him. This could have meant that his schizophrenia and psychosis may have been caused by the drugs that he had previously consumed.

One day, nurses found him with blood around his mouth, they discovered two dead and mutilated birds outside his window that he had lured for capture. It's quite clear that Chase suffered from a mental disorder early on in his life, brought on by physical abuse and humiliation.

He may also have been suffering from Renfield Syndrome, a form of clinical vampirism. After two stints inside the psychiatric hospitals, he was released in late 1976 after being deemed no longer a risk to society. How wrong they were.

He was able to move into another apartment in the city and restarted trapping cats and dogs to kill and consume. In his trial, his mother claimed that Chase appeared on her doorstep one day with a dead cat.

He smiled, threw the cat to the ground and ripped it open with his bare hands. Then he smeared the animal's blood all over his neck and face. In an even more bizarre chain of events, his mother failed to contact anyone over the incident.

This was only a few years before he would kill his human victims and drink their blood in a misconstrued belief that he was keeping himself alive. It was because he believed Nazi's had carried out invasive experiments on him causing him to physically need the blood.

Chase was to become synonymous with the term of serial killer. His monstrous crimes are still talked about, discussed, and used as a basis for television shows to this very day. When some people think of serial killers, they might think of schizophrenic individuals who as a child had a tendency for killing small animals and acting bizarrely. Chase fitted every profile available at the time.

From animals to humans

On 29th December 1977, Chase killed Ambrose Griffin, a 51-year-old engineer in the city. After a shopping trip, Griffin returned to his car to get the last of the items. When his wife stepped back outside, she saw her husband on the ground next to the grocery bags. Chase had shot him twice. In hindsight, it was a trial run for darker killings.

One month later, on the evening of 23rd January 1978, Chase attempted to break into a house at 2909 Burnece Street. When a neighbour approached him, he stopped, lit a cigarette, stared at her and casually walked away. That same night, he broke into a house along the street but was interrupted by the owners and he ran off, but not before smearing his excrement on some of their belongings.

He moved down the street to 2360 Tioga Way and casually walked into the home of the Wallin family.

He bumped into Teresa Wallin as she was taking out the garbage. Chase shot her three times and dragged her corpse to the bedroom leaving a blood trail through the house. He raped her corpse whilst stabbing her multiple times with a kitchen knife.

Chase then proceeded to carve off her left nipple and cut her torso open below the sternum. He removed her spleen and intestines, cut out her kidneys and sliced her pancreas in half. He then placed the kidneys back inside the body as if they were one organ.

He used a yogurt pot to scoop up the blood from inside her body and drink it. He would then rub her blood over his face and neck. Before he left the house, Chase had gone into the garden, picked up some dog excrement and pushed it into her throat and mouth.

The extreme brutality of the Walling murder was to shock not just California, but the whole of the United States. The media got wind of the story and as the killer seemed to have a fascination with drinking blood, Chase earned the dubious title of 'Vampire of Sacramento'.

Unending blood lust

Four days later, and just one mile from the Wallin house, the Miroth family would suffer a similar, if not worse fate. Chase entered the Miroth residence and shot dead a family friend named Danny Meredith. He stole his wallet and car keys before rampaging through the home.

He shot and killed 38-year-old Evelyn Miroth, her six-year-old son, Jason Miroth, and her 22-month-old nephew, David Ferreira. He raped Evelyn's corpse, cut her open and took some of her organs out before drinking her blood direct from the body. His desire for vampirism and necrophilia had left nothing to the imagination.

The investigation moved forward very quickly. Chase hadn't tried to hide what he had done. Evidence was easy to come by and when they searched his apartment they found everything they needed to charge, but it wasn't as if they needed to look that hard.

Everything in the kitchen was blood stained, from the fridge to the drinking glasses. One container had pieces of brain fragments and others had small pieces of bone within them. The electric blender had never been cleaned and contained a mixture of blood from numerous animals.

Before his trial, it was claimed Chase virtually turned into an animal when they tried to extract blood from him for a sample. He was subsequently charged with six counts of murder in the first degree, it was a trial that was to last four months during the course of 1978.

On 8th May 1979, after only a few hours, the jury returned the obvious verdict of guilty of six counts of murder in the first degree. He was given the death penalty by gas chamber at San Quentin Prison.

Nazi UFOs and a powdered heart

Chase gave a series of bizarre interviews in which he spoke of his fear of Nazis and UFOs. He believed he had been secretly killed by a combination of both, reanimated, and forced to kill others in order to keep himself alive. He asked the interviewer, FBI Agent Robert Ressler for a radar gun, so that he could capture the Nazi UFOs and bring them to justice for the murders.

Chase's delusions also led him to believe that his blood was turning to powder and that he needed blood from other creatures to replenish it, as his heart was shrinking. He was to begin an appeal on the basis that he was only killing to preserve his own life.

Needless to say that Chase would go onto become the poster boy for a paranoid schizophrenic serial killer and the type of killer your parents would warn you about before you went to sleep. He was also feared by other prisoners due to the extremely violent nature of his crimes.

On Boxing Day 1980, a guard found him dead in his cell. He had committed suicide with an overdose of antidepressants that he had collected and saved. When Chase's body was autopsied, it was found that his heart was in a perfectly healthy condition.

THE BRAZILIAN BLOOD-DRINKER

Marcelo Costa de Andrade, the Vampire of Niterói, killed at least 14 young boys before drinking their blood to maintain his youthful appearance.

'I sawed off his head so that the children would make fun of him when he arrived in heaven.'

Thus the world was introduced to one of the most violent vampiric serial killers in history, Marcelo Costa de Andrade, AKA: The Vampire of Niterói. The above quote refers to the murder of an 11-year-old boy, who Marcelo lured from a soccer field.

He strangled the boy into unconsciousness before raping him, not knowing if he was dead or alive.

He then proceeded to sever the boys head from his body before leaving him to be found by his friends. And it was not the first time Marcelo had committed atrocities against young boys.

Marcelo was born in January 1967 into an existence marred by darkness and abuse. He was born in Rocinha, the largest and most populous favela in Brazil, settled into the hillside overlooking Rio de Janeiro's South Zone. It is home to over 200,000 people.

His mother was regularly beaten and abused by his father, and he was forced to watch. When family members found out, he was sent to his grandparents' home where he had a couple of years of normal upbringing.

When his grandparents aged and were unable to look after him, and at the age of ten, he was sent back to his mother and father, where the abuse had escalated. The family home was constantly full of his father's companions, some of whom abused Marcelo, including an older man who raped him on multiple occasions.

Sending children to Heaven.

Marcelo was admitted to a boy's school shelter in Rio but his grades were poor and due to the abuse, he had become withdrawn from society. Other boys bullied him for being 'retarded' and he was mistreated by some of the older boys.

He remained in the shelter until the age of 14, when he became too old to be homed there. He was kicked out and left to fend for himself. To get by, he turned to prostitution and was regularly visited by an older man who forced him to submit.

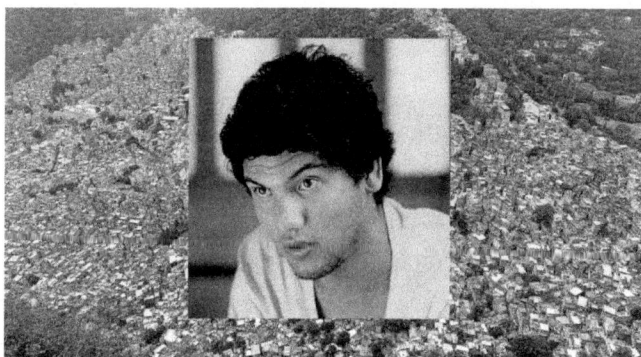

Two years later, at the age of 16, he lived with an older gay man who introduced him to the Christian Church. Only a year later, he raped a ten-year-old boy but the boy refused to identify him and he got away with it.

He carried on visiting the church he had been introduced to and did so for the next eight years. But when he was not practicing the word of God, he was reading and collecting pornographic magazines. He also took an unusual liking to children's TV shows and songs.

In one of the services at the church, he heard that when children die they go to Heaven. Adults would either go to Heaven or Hell, depending on how they had lived their lives and whether or not they had repented for any sins. But in Marcelo's head, it meant he could kill children as they would go straight to heaven. It meant he had the power to send children to Heaven.

Perfect cover to kill.

In April 1991, when he was 24, Marcelo left the relationship he was in and returned to his family home. Then he embarked on a nine-month killing spree that would come to shock the world. Not only because of the murders, but because of what he did to his victims, and the drinking of their blood.

Bolstered by the belief he would not kill adults, as he could be sending them to Hell, he looked towards young boys as victims. During this time, despite his sexual preferences, he was deemed a perfectly normal human being. But there was a vampiric tendency at his heart that could not be quelled.

It was perhaps a sad state of affairs that many thousands of children went missing from the favelas surrounding Rio, and still do to this day. Hundreds more are murdered each year. It is perhaps no surprise that Marcelo was able to get away with murdering at least 14 boys.

By 1991, at least four children were being executed every single day in an enforcement mission to clean up the streets. Marcelo had the perfect cover to act on his vampiric desires and take children from the streets to their deaths.

He later admitted that sometimes he was unsure if his victims were dead or not before he raped them and drank their blood. But it didn't matter to him as he was happy he was able to send children to Heaven, to escape the hell of the favelas.

Drinking blood to stay young.

He later claimed his killing spree was kickstarted when a 14-year-old transvestite propositioned him for sex. He went to a hotel with them and paid the equivalent of £10 to have sex for an afternoon. He claimed the trans was so soft and supple that he wanted to experience it again. When he couldn't track the boy down, he turned to forcing himself on younger boys.

His first victim was a street urchin, a child who spent most of the time on the streets partaking in petty crime, as were most of his victims. He lured the unsuspecting boy to an isolated area in the hills surrounding Rio by asking him to help light some candles for the church.

When there was no one around, he strangled him to death with his own t-shirt before raping the corpse. He returned to the body every day for three days to see if it had been discovered but it hadn't. With all the violence going on in the favelas, nobody suspected a child rapist and blood drinker among them.

All of his victims were between the ages of six and thirteen. On one occasion, he crushed a boy's head with a rock, then scooped out the blood in his hands and drank it. Marcelo had come to believe that if he drank the blood of his victims, he would become as youthful as they were.

He made sure the boys were aged 13 and under. On some occasions, after raping them, he would slice their arteries and drink blood directly from the body. Either from the wrists, neck, or occasionally from the genital area.

'I preferred young boys because they are better looking and have soft skin. And the priest said that children automatically go to heaven if they die before they're thirteen.

So I know I did them a favour by sending them to heaven.'
Such was Marcelo's reasoning for the murders.

Bowl of blood.

For the next nine months, he continued to lure young boys to their deaths. He would offer them sweets or money, and most accepted, though he later admitted some of the older boys ignored him – which only made him seek out younger boys.

He abused one victim for an entire night before cracking his head open with a rock and collecting the blood in bowl. Before the sun rose the following day, he drank the blood from the bowl and later buried the boy in a shallow grave.

The bowl went with Marcelo everywhere, including to church, which he still visited, despite becoming a demon of his own making. He used the bowl on many occasions to drink the blood of his victims, stating it was sometimes easier than drinking it direct from the arteries.

He began to believe he was possessed by an evil spirit, as the church constantly pointed out that homosexuality was a disease. Because of his 'disease' he had allowed a demonic entity to enter him, one that had a desire for children's blood.

He didn't kill young girls because he thought boys were softer and prettier. He also came to believe that only young boys went to Heaven, and that it was different for girls, though he never offered an explanation why.

Chopping off the head.

One victim was 11-year-old Odair Jose Muniz, who Marcelo lured from a soccer pitch to an isolated area of woodland. He raped and killed Muniz and left his body in the open but returned in the early hours of the morning with a machete.

Upon finding the body undisturbed, he cut off the boy's head and left it near the torso. When he was interviewed in 2001 by Helen Morrison, an American criminal psychiatrist, Marcelo said of the murder: '*I sawed off his head so that the children would make fun of him when he arrived in heaven.*'

On 11th December, Marcelo lured 10-year-old Altair Abreu and his six-year-old brother Ivan to an isolated area close to the church. He attempted to kiss Altair who tried to run but was thrown to the ground. Marcelo then raped and killed Ivan in front of him.

He then told Altair he had sent his brother to Heaven, and by doing so, he had fallen in love with

Altair. He took such a liking to the young boy, that he wasn't worried when Altair escaped and ran back home to his mother.

Marcelo was arrested two days later while handing out flyers for the church. He was charged with Ivan's murder, but after police interviewed his mother, they learned there could have been more victims.

The untreatable vampire.

His mother told them of the machete, his blood-stained bowl, and the fact he had come home covered in blood on more than one occasion. Living in the favelas, she had put it down to fighting or drug-related crime.

The truth was that Marcelo had been on a nine-month killing spree which had gone under the radar. Had Altair not escaped then the number of victims would have been much higher. When interviewed by police, Marcelo confessed to the other 13 murders and led them to the burial sites.

He was eventually declared insane and sentenced to life in a maximum-security psychiatric hospital. He was interviewed by many serial killer experts over the years, with one, Ilana Casoy, stating he was the most terrifying person she had ever met.

It materialised during their conversations that Marcelo had kept the shorts of his victims as trophies. He came across as someone childlike in nature, with no real understanding of what he had done, and the mind of a 12-year-old.

For a while, Ilana struggled to comprehend he was the person who carried out the murders. Until a sickening revelation, when Marcelo asked Ilana to bring a pair of boys shorts to him on her next visit, to which she refused, and never returned.

She confirmed that the medical staff at the hospital have no idea how to treat him, so they keep him sedated with drugs. Despite an escape and recapture in 1997, Marcelo remains under psychiatric care to this day.

Serial killers are rare in Brazil, and vampires, more so. Marcelo is one of the only known South American vampiric serial killers. He became known as the Vampire of Niterói and is said to keep an empty bowl with him in his room.

VAMPIRE KILLER COUPLE

When a German Satanist found his Princess of Darkness, they embarked on a journey through Vampirism, which ended in the murder of their friend, as a sacrifice to Satan.

One vampire is disturbing enough but when two dark souls cross paths and share a capacity for sickness, there's no telling the lengths they will go to. German-born Daniel Ruda was a self-confessed vampire – and car parts salesman – who was looking for the missing part of his soul.

When Daniel was a child, he was known to be withdrawn and often flinched at physical contact, leading some to suspect he was abused but it has never been proven. During his teens he found a love of black metal and gothic culture but went to extremes not often found in the community.

He joined an underground German gothic community where other gothic extremists practiced Satanic rituals and drank each other's blood. He and his friends would often cut themselves then drink directly from each other.

In his early twenties, he became involved in the neo-Nazi movement which had gained traction in Germany in the late 1990s. When it fizzled out, he joined a black metal band which only lasted a few months.

In 2000, at the age of 23, he fully embraced Satanism as a life choice and came to believe he had been chosen as Satan's messenger. To help spread the word and share his desires, he needed to find the female version of himself.

To find the perfect match, he placed an advert in the classifieds of a heavy metal magazine It read: *'Black-haired vampire seeks princess of darkness who despises everything and everybody and has bidden farewell to life.'* Then he sat back and waited for a reply – and he didn't have to wait long.

Princess of Darkness.

20-year-old German national, Manuela Bartel, responded to the advert with a resounding yes. Manuela was also looking for her dark soulmate, one to share the delights of Satan with, and she had been practicing for longer than Daniel.

At the age of 13, she was arrested for biting pedestrians in the street. She was also known to crawl on the ground in an attempt to bite people's ankles. She was seen multiple times by a psychiatrist but never admitted to hospital.

Daniel Ruda in court for murder.

In the three years that followed, her condition deteriorated. She believed Satan had been trying to contact her through her dreams and had visions during her waking hours. Unable to control the onslaught, she left school and overdosed on drugs.

She survived but decided to run away from Germany at the age of 16 and move to England.

She got work at a goth club in London and managed to get by with help from new friends. There, she met like-minded people following the vampiric lifestyle and became involved in bloodletting.

It was to her, an education in vampirism, as London has always been known for its underground goth culture, where extremists are allowed to hide. She shared her blood and drank the blood of others before realising she needed time alone.

She went to work at a hotel on the Isle of Skye, Scotland. It closed during the Winter months but she was allowed to board there. The minimal daylight and deep cloud cover of the Western Isles during the Winter felt like home. She enjoyed the dark atmosphere, claiming that sunlight hurt her eyes.

Before she replied to Daniel's advert, she wrote a letter to a man who lived in a hut on the Isle of Skye. His name was Tom Leppard, a man in his sixties known as The Leopard Man, for having his entire body tattooed in Leopard spots.

She lived with him for many months but decided he wasn't for her. In 1998, she returned home to Germany where she worked in goth clubs. In 2000, Manuela saw the ad from Daniel and decided to reply to him.

Manuela Ruda in court for murder.

A vision from Satan.

Around the same time, Manuela went to a Satanic ceremony where she pledged her soul to Satan. She had two teeth removed and vampire fangs put into their place. After shaving the hair on both sides of her head, she had an inverted cross tattooed on her temple.

Psychiatrists later suggested if they had not met, they might have grown out of their love of Satanism naturally and individually. But as it was, the crossing of two dark souls brought their vampiric tendencies to the forefront of everything they did.

They embraced vampire culture completely, even going as far as sleeping in coffins during the day. They holidayed in England and Scotland, sleeping in graveyards and attending Satanic parties, preferring the gloomy atmosphere of the countries.

Daniel then had a vision from Satan. It told him to marry Manuela on 6th June 2001, then kill a human being exactly one month later. By doing so, they would be allowed into Hell.

After marrying in a civil ceremony, they turned their attention to completing Satan's order. One of their friend's from the goth clubs was a 33-year-old man named Frank Hackert, who once worked with Daniel at the car parts garage.

The couple enjoyed Frank's company as they found him funny and likeable. It meant he would make a perfect court jester for Satan when they sent him to Hell. On 6th July 2011, Frank was invited to the Ruda's home for a party – and would never leave alive.

Drinking the blood of the sacrifice.

The only problem was, Frank was the only guest. Soon after he arrived, the Ruda's claimed Satan had taken possession of them to help carry out the slaying. Daniel hit Frank on the back of the head with a hammer, crushing his skull with many blows.

He then stabbed him multiple times before laying him on the coffin they used as a coffee table. Still alive, Frank coughed up blood but couldn't move. Manuela then claimed the moonlight shone onto a knife sitting on the windowsill.

She took it and plunged it into Frank's heart. The pair then used a variety of instruments to stab Frank's corpse, including a carpet cutter, scalpel and machete. They carved a pentagram into his chest and collected the blood into a bowl before drinking from it together in the moonlight. But Lady and the Tramp this was not.

The couple had planned to kill themselves after the murder but decided against it and instead drove around Germany, waiting for Satan to reward them. Police arrived at their home the following day after Manuela's mother received a suicide note but nothing prepared them for what they saw.

One officer likened the murder scene to something from a Cannibal Corpse album cover, a band notorious for gruesome artwork. The scalpel was still sticking out of Frank's chest and the bloodstained bowl sat beside him. A piece of paper with the words '*When Satan Lives*' had been placed beside the body.

Daniel and Manuela in the months before the murder.

The devil made them do it.

Five days after the murder, on July 12th, the couple were arrested in the city of Jena and went willingly with police. The trial began in early 2002. Both turned up at court dressed in black goth clothing. The defence lawyers requested the windows be covered as Manuela had an aversion to daylight. The judge refused but allowed her to wear black sunglasses.

Both showed no remorse during the trial. They interrupted proceedings constantly, made funny faces, bared their teeth, and laughed at the victim's family. The couple were found guilty of murder but the judge deemed them to have personality disorders.

The pair claimed they had not killed anyone, as they were carrying out an order to sacrifice a human for Satan. They were simply doing Satan's work and could not be held responsible for their ultimate actions.

At the trial, Daniel said, '*if I kill a person with a car and half his bleeding head is hanging on the radiator grille, the car is not put on trial, the driver is the bad one. I have no reason to regret anything because I have not done anything.*' Manuela simply stated, '*I signed my soul to Satan two-and-a-half years ago.*'

Manuela was sentenced to 13 years in a psychiatric prison. She has since been released back into society under a new identity. Daniel was sentenced to 16 years. He was released in 2017 and his whereabouts are currently unknown. He often spoke of moving to England or Scotland, but no one knows.

For the victim's family, who fought for a life sentence, their release had proved difficult. With Frank's father recorded as saying, '*he (Daniel) will be walking into a bright future and I will only be walking into the cemetery to visit my son.'*

Daniel and Manuela believed they were vampires on a mission handed down from Satan. Their reward for following Satan was a hefty prison sentence and many lives ruined. They claimed the devil made them do it but they used the dark one as an excuse to commit murder – and build a hell for themselves.

"If you want to find a Vampire
YOU'LL NEED A 7-YEAR-OLD BOY
AND A WHITE HORSE."

- Romanian Legend

VAMPIRE OF HANOVER

A German butcher was praised for his cheap meat prices, until it was discovered he had been killing young boys by biting into their necks and drinking their blood, before selling their flesh to unsuspecting customers.

There is a fine line between vampirism and cannibalism as both involve the consumption of parts of the human body. They are mostly differentiated between the drinking of blood for vampires, and the eating of human flesh for cannibals.

Some cannibals drink human blood but are not labelled as vampires because they also consume human flesh. Vampires do not. Which brings us nicely onto Fritz Haarmann, who 100 years ago, killed and mutilated at least 24 young boys in the city of Hanover, Germany.

Described as the most revolting case in German criminal history.

Haarmann was born in 1879, the youngest of six children, and was known to be withdrawn from an early age. It was in stark contrast to his siblings, who were lively and sociable. He often dressed up in his sister's clothes and played with their dolls.

His mother was adoring of him, and his father distant but strict, a womaniser who had affairs with multiple women during his marriage. Haarmann managed to escape his working-class roots and enrolled in a military academy at the age of 15 in 1895.

He grew into a strong, physically domineering character but his military career was cut short when he began passing out due to epilepsy-like conditions, though it was never diagnosed. A year later, when he was 16, Haarmann committed his first criminal offence – a sign of the horrors to come.

A damaged mind.

In the year following his discharge from the academy, he began luring young boys to isolated areas before sexually abusing and raping them. After his arrest in 1896, he was sent to a psychiatric institution for evaluation and was found unfit to stand trial.

He remained in the unit until January 1898, when he escaped with the help of his mother who still doted on her youngest child. She helped him escape to Switzerland where he lived with distant family members and worked in a shipyard.

The psychiatric evaluation period had lapsed which meant there was no legal need to return him to the unit. He returned to Hanover, married a woman named Erna Loewert, and had a child with her. But in 1900, he was ordered into compulsory military service, despite being kicked out years earlier.

Fritz Haarmann, the Vampire of Hanover.

He survived two years in the service and became an exemplary soldier but in 1902 he passed out again while on routine exercise and was discharged. The discharge made him angry, as he later claimed the second stint in the military was the best of his life.

It was an anger that simmered beneath the surface, and with no military rule to follow, he began to drift into lawlessness. Despite receiving a pension from the military, he went to work in his father's cigar factory but got into a violent fight with him following his mother's death.

His father tried to have him charged for the attack, claiming his son belonged in a mental institution but the charges were dropped due to a lack of evidence. After flittering from job to job, he opened a fishmongers with Erna but she had an affair with a student and kicked him out of her life and business.

It was the final catalyst, the last curtain before the veil finally dropped.

Biting their necks.

For the next ten years, he turned to a life of crime, including gravedigging and the robbing of tombstones. From 1905 to 1918, he served various short-term prison sentences for robbery and fraud. At the same time, he came out as gay and had casual relationships with other men.

By the end of 1918, due to his extensive criminal career, Haarmann had become a police informant but used the position to deflect attention away from his own crimes. He was allowed to patrol Hanover Train Station with no interference from police – an opportunity to act on his dark desires.

His first murder victim was 17-year-old Friedel Rothe, a runaway who headed to Hanover. Haarmann lured him back to his apartment with the promise of temporary accommodation and food. When his sexual advances were rejected, Haarmann bared his teeth and bit into Rothe's neck, tearing the Adam's apple off.

He then strangled the boy to death. It was a method used to kill many of his victims. Most would die from the severing of the arteries caused by Haarmann's bite and would choke on their own blood. If he saw they were still alive a few minutes later, he finished them off with strangulation.

Rothe was last seen with Haarmann, and police were forced to investigate. They arrived at his apartment to find him involved in a sexual liaison with a 13-year-old boy. Little did they know, that Rothe's head was hidden behind his cooker, wrapped in newspaper.

The love bite.

He received a sentence of nine months in prison for being with the 13-year-old and served out his sentence by the end of 1920. Around the same time, he met one of his lovers, Hans Grans, a former convict who had run away from home. Grans was bisexual and a pimp to female sex workers.

They moved into a ground floor apartment in a densely populated residential block, overcrowded due to the fallout of the war. Haarmann later claimed to have loved Hans, but his love, as always, was never reciprocated. They went their separate ways after Grans became concerned over his attraction to young boys.

During the final months of their relationship, Haarmann picked up 17-year-old Fritz Franke and took him back to the apartment. A day later, Grans had returned home to see Fritz's nude body on the bed and assumed Haarmann was in the middle of a casual encounter.

What Grans didn't know, was that Fritz's neck had been ripped apart by Haarmann's teeth and he would have been looking at a dead body. By June 1923, Haarmann moved out of the basement apartment and into a single attic room, where he had more privacy to kill and dismember his victims.

The address at 2 Rote Reihe, became notorious with the murders, and was a place where

Haarmann's crimes escalated. Between 1918 and 1924, he killed at least 24 young boys and men but claimed most of his victims in the attic flat from 1923 to 1924.

He later referred to his method of murder as a love bite. With the victims he killed by biting through the neck, he admitted that he also drank their blood, as they lay thrashing beneath him. He also engaged in necrophilia and sexually abused the corpses long after they had left the world of the living.

All of his victims were dismembered before either being spread around the city – or sold as meat!

Fritz Haarmann's attic room, photographed during the investigation.

A very specific process of dismemberment.

He had a very specific way in which he dismembered his victims but never drank dead blood, preferring only to drink it direct from the body when it was warm. He admitted he killed for the thrill and the blood but disliked the process of dismemberment – despite it being necessary in his eyes.

After a strong coffee laced with alcohol, he placed the nude body on the floor and covered the face before slicing into the lower torso and removing the intestines. To stop the blood flowing from the body, he squashed towels into the cavity to soak it up.

After slicing through the meat of the ribs, he pushed on the bones until the shoulders broke, allowing him easy access to the organs. He placed the heart, lungs, kidneys, and liver into a bucket with the intestines, before severing the arms and legs.

With the limbs separated, he sliced the remaining flesh from the bones. He kept the good parts for the bucket and either flushed the rest down the toilet or disposed of it with the bones in the nearby river.

The final part of the dismemberment was the head. He used a sharp kitchen knife to remove all the flesh from the skull, then placed it on a pile of straw and bludgeoned it until the skull became small pieces of bone. He wrapped the pieces in a rag with the brain and dropped it in the local river with the rest.

Except, he kept the bucket of organs and some of the flesh, not for his own personal enjoyment but for financial gain. He ground most of the organs up and made sausages with them. With the larger parts of flesh, he made cutlets to look like beef or pork.

Due to his knowledge of Hanover Station and his informer status with the police, he was able to sell the sausages and cutlets on the black market. The unsuspecting customers were simply thrilled to find meat, as post-war Germany temporarily struggled with the meat industry.

Little did the customers know that the sausages were made out of human flesh.

Over 500 human bones.

In May of 1924, two macabre discoveries were made that would eventually lead to Haarmann. The first was when two young children playing near the River Leine uncovered a human skull on the banks. Two weeks later, another skull with knife wounds was found in a water channel next to a water wheel.

In early June, two young boys playing near the river's edge in the local village came across a sack full of bones. By that point, police were certain a disturbing serial killer was at work in the city of Hanover, and unless they did something, he wouldn't be stopped.

Over the previous six years, police were aware of a disproportionate number of young boys and men who had gone missing and were last seen near Hanover Station. The sheer number suggested the killer had claimed more victims, and they decided to dredge the riverbed.

Within a week, they had discovered over 500 human bones belonging to at least 22 different people. Suspicions immediately fell on Haarmann due to his previous convictions and his informer position at Hanover Station.

Because he knew many of the police in Hanover, two undercover officers were drafted in from Berlin to keep him under surveillance, which began in late June 1924. They watched him argue with a 15-year-old boy named Karl Fromm. Haarmann dragged him to police at the station and told them to arrest Karl due to having forged documents.

But Karl told police he had been kept in Haarmann's attic room for four days and had been raped multiple times at knifepoint. Haarmann was arrested and charged with rape, which gave police the opportunity to search the attic flat.

Fritz Haarmann (the man with no hat) with police investigators in November 1924.

Beheading the vampire.

The walls, floor, and ceiling were extensively bloodstained but Haarmann claimed it was due to his involvement in the black market meat trade – which wasn't a lie. But former tenants gave statements to the police about the great number of different young boys who had gone into the attic room, and the many sacks and buckets Haarmann would bring out.

A bigger search of the apartment found clothing belonging to many of the missing boys. Haarmann claimed the clothing had come from meat trades or left by the young men he had casual experiences with.

But the evidence was stacking up and Haarmann finally confessed to some of the murders. He said he had an insatiable urge to bite the necks of his victims and drink their blood from the neck. It was a desire he could not control but was unable to say when the urge had first appeared.

Haarmann only confessed to the murders where there was evidence against him. When asked how many he had killed, he said '*somewhere between 50 and 70.*' He was ultimately linked with 27 disappearances and 24 murders.

Hans Grans was later arrested as an accessory to one of the murders and ultimately sentenced to 12 years after a retrial. But it was Haarmann who grabbed headlines across the world. The trial began in December 1924 and lasted less than two weeks.

The amount of evidence against Haarmann was overwhelming and he was convicted of 24 murders. His sentence: death by beheading. At 6am on 15th April 1925, Haarmann was beheaded by a guillotine at Hanover Prison.

And so ended the tale of one of Germany's most disturbing criminals. He is known today as the

Vampire of Hanover, a fitting moniker for someone who killed on an urge to bite his victims necks and drink their blood.

"Condemn me to death. Deliver me from this life, which is a torment. I will not petition for mercy, nor will I appeal. I want to pass just one more merry night in my cell, with coffee, cheese and cigars, after which I will curse my father and go to my execution as if it were a wedding."

Fritz Haarmann addressing the court prior to his sentencing. December 1924.

MARSHFIELD VAMPIRE KILLER

A man believing he was a 700-year-old vampire shot dead his grandmother with gold bullets and drank her blood, claiming he needed the blood of his elders to survive.

Marshfield in Plymouth County, Massachusetts, is probably best known as the home of Daniel Webster, the U.S. Secretary of State from 1850 to 1852. The town doubles in population during the Summer due to its enviable coastal location.

On 10th April 1980 during a cold Spring, a 700-year-old vampire visited the home of 74-year-old disabled pensioner Carmen Lopez and ended her life. The perpetrator was her grandson, 23-year-old James P. Riva, who would come to be known as The Schizophrenic Vampire or the Marshfield Vampire Killer.

James had lived with wheelchair-bound Carmen for the past nine months since the Summer of 1979. Just days before the murder, he moved out and shacked up with Henry Lopez, his granduncle. On the day of the murder, it appeared to many that James was living a normal day, like any other.

Henry drove James to his father's home in Braintree, eighteen miles away, where James claimed he was going for a job interview. When Henry drove away, James borrowed his father's car and went back to Marshfield.

There, he drove to an auto supply store where he bumped into an old high-school teacher. He asked the teacher about how to fix brake linings. It seemed a usual thing to ask for but the teacher began to get bad vibes from him and made their excuses to leave.

At 3pm, he parked on a road a couple of blocks away from Carmen's home and went in through the front door. He found her lying on the couch. She asked him to do some washing for her. But less than half hour later, Carmen was dead.

Sucking blood from the bullet holes.

James had constantly argued with his grandmother about his long hair and lack of employment, going as far to call him useless. On that afternoon, James followed her instructions and began to sort out the washing.

Halfway through, he left the chore and retrieved four gold-painted bullets and a gun from the cellar, which he had previously stored down there. Carmen saw the gun and threw a glass at him. Angered by her hate, James shot her then stabbed her to make sure she was dead.

As she sat dying in her wheelchair, James dropped to his knees and began drinking the blood from the wounds. He sucked the blood out of the bullet holes because a vampire had told him to do so.

You see, James had come to believe he was a 700-year-old vampire, as revealed to him by the voice of an unidentified vampire in his head. He learned that to remain youthful, he needed to drink the fresh blood of his elders, and his grandmother was the perfect victim, for they never really got along.

For many months, James desired human and animal blood to the point that he would sometimes roam the countryside attempting to catch animals to kill. He was also known to eat sporadically and choose shop-bought animal blood as food. He later admitted to killing a horse and drinking the blood from its neck.

Photo of James P. Riva taken in court.

Brain on fire.

After he drank much of Carmen's blood, he carried her into the bedroom and set her on fire. Before he left the house, he rolled the wheelchair into her bedroom, to make it look like a freak accident. A painter working on a neighbour's house saw the flames and called emergency services.

The fire service arrived and extinguished the flames. When they found Carmen's body in the bedroom, the police were called in. By which point, James was picking up his father in Braintree and bringing him back to Marshfield.

As they drove back to his grandmother's house, he confessed he had been inside the property earlier in the day but had trouble remembering entirely what happened. He was arrested the moment he returned to the house.

James had a well-documented history of mental illness and had been admitted to various psychiatric institutes from a young age. One psychiatrist had previously diagnosed him with paranoid schizophrenia, a disorder associated with hallucinations and delusions.

While awaiting his trial, his estranged mother, Janet Jones, visited him on many occasions. He allegedly told her that his brain was on fire and his stomach hurt due to a lack of fresh blood. He also claimed the vampire talking to him in his head was becoming aggressive towards him.

Criminally responsible.

During the trial, there were further revelations of the life James lived and what led him to becoming the Marshfield Vampire. There were accusations his mother had severely abused him as a child. At first she denied the claims but wrote a letter to the court confessing she had sinned against him.

When James was a child, she would repeatedly dunk his head in a sink of water, threatening to drown him. She also beat him for not carrying out chores or for simply not being the boy she had wanted from the beginning.

A defence psychiatrist spoke of his conversations with James. Though he claimed he was a 700-year-old vampire, he believed he had come from a long line of vampires, and that his grandmother was working to suppress his vampirism.

He said that she would prick him with an ice pick in order to draw blood away from his body, before attempting to drink it. It was an apparent ritual if an elder vampire wanted to halt the growth of a younger one.

Despite the mental disorders and many psychiatric evaluations claiming James to be extremely ill, he was found criminally responsible for the murder. The trial lasted only a few weeks. James was found guilty of murder and sentenced to life in prison.

Confined until death.

In the years that followed, James was admitted to a nearby psychiatric unit four times and was diagnosed again with schizophrenia and personality disorder. While in prison, he allegedly held down a job in the hopes of achieving parole.

In 2009, at a second parole board hearing, his lawyer spoke of James' willingness to re-join society. He had been on mental health medication for nearly three decades by that point and claimed to be sorry for his actions.

However, the board refused to grant James his freedom. Members of the board felt he couldn't be trusted, showed limited or false remorse, and lacked insight into the cause of his violence. They concluded he would be unfit for re-entry into society.

Their conclusion was bolstered by the revelation that he was found to be writing threatening letters to his mother, in which he wrote of drinking her blood. He had also attacked one of the prison guards with a shiv and beat him with a mop handle, accusing him of sneaking into his cell to drain his spinal fluid.

One board member proclaimed, *'god forbid if he got loose in society again. Somebody would die.'* His most recent parole hearing was in 2019, when he was 62. Again, he was denied and is due for another hearing in 2024, aged 66.

The Marshfield Vampire Killer was years in the making from a damaged childhood to a broken mind. Despite all the psychiatric help he has received, it appears he – or the 700-year-old vampire within him – will remain confined until his death.

KISS OF THE VAMPIRE

A Vampiric serial killer named Béla Kiss drained the blood of 24 victims and pickled their bodies in metal drums – before escaping capture and falling into the realm of mythology.

Born in Izsak, Hungary, in 1877, the unusually named Bela Kiss had a tempestuous upbringing. Records show he was having an incestuous relationship with his mother, Verona Varga, though there was no real evidence in it. And yet, it could explain the bizarre route that Bela took in life.

From a tinsmith to a vampiric serial killer, Bela would go on to claim the lives of at least 23 women and one man. He killed over an 11-year-period from 1903 to 1914 until he was drafted to fight in the First World War.

When he was presumed dead in the war, his landlord visited the property and uncovered horrors never before seen in the country. His victims had been drained of blood, had bite marks on their necks, and their corpses were being pickled in large metal drums.

Bela was considered to have been a handsome man with blond hair and bright blue eyes, a catch for any young woman. He left Izsak in his teens and moved to the town of Cinkota, which is now a suburb of Budapest close to the River Danube.

He taught himself how to become a tinsmith and built a reputable business making and repairing items of tin or other light metals. In 1900, he moved to a large property in the suburb suitable for his daily work – and the life he had built for himself in the shadows.

The solicitation of victims.

Bela had two failed marriages and two children, who were ignorant of what he was doing in the barn and throughout the night. As he focused more on his work, his wives had enough and left him for greener pastures. But Bela wasn't short of women, thanks to his new occult pastime.

In 1912, after his second wife left him for a younger man, Bela hired a housekeeper named Mrs. Jakubec, who began to notice something unusual about her new employer. She discovered that Bela had become a fortune teller and was offering occult services to the local villagers and further afield to the city folk.

Jakubec began to notice single women turning up at the home to meet with Bela for his services or to go on a date, but really, he was seeking victims. He solicited the women through the classified sections of local and national newspapers.

Some of the women who went to his home disappeared forever and he was the last person to see them alive. You see, Bela had an ulterior motive in bringing women to his home. He wanted to drink their blood.

Perfected victim selection.

He managed to remain under the radar for so long due to the set-up he had perfected. When his tinsmith business took off, he had enough money to hire an apartment in Budapest, where most of the newspaper advertisements were placed.

First, the women would visit the apartment then Bela would convince them to travel with him to his home in Cinkota. It either happened the same day or at a later date. Due to his occult associations, his victims didn't tell others where they were going, and by siphoning his victims to his rural home, he had perfected his victim selection.

No questions were asked, and the victims were never linked to him. Despite Jakubec noticing many women entering the Cinkota home, she only put it down to Bela being an eligible bachelor, taking his time to select his perfect match – or playing the single life.

She also didn't question the large number of metal drums that surrounded the property, due to Bela's business. Because of the impending war in Europe, many homeowners were stockpiling their own oil and gas, so metal drums were not an uncommon sight.

In 1914, Bela was drafted into the First World War but Jakubec was kept on in a part-time capacity. In July 1916, rumours began circulating that Bela had been killed in action or had been taken as a prisoner of war.

The owner of the land on which the property was set, saw a financial opportunity and decided to put the old Bela house up for sale. He went to the property and noticed the metal drums outside. After piercing one with a knife, a vomit-inducing smell emanated from within it – the unmistakeable aroma of human decomposition.

Preserved corpses.

The landlord contacted one of Budapest's top detectives, a Dr. Charles Nagy, who arrived within hours accompanied by two younger officers. Charles opened the first drum to find a horrifying sight inside – the preserved body of a young woman with brown hair.

Also present in the drum was the rope with which she had been strangled to death. Her body had been preserved with methanol, a wood alcohol, commonly used as a precursor to the preserving agent formaldehyde.

Six more drums were opened and six more bodies were found inside, in various states of decomposition. Charles ordered the entire site to be cordoned off and searched. He then sent communication to the military that if Bela Kiss were alive, then he was to be arrested immediately for multiple murders.

Jakubec was arrested as an accomplice but quickly released after it became apparent she knew nothing of what was going on. She told them of the women she had seen coming to and from the home but beyond that she was ignorant to the extent of the crimes.

She showed the detective to Bela's bedroom, which she had kept in pristine condition since he had left for the war. The room contained no evidence but Charles noticed a secret door with a lock on it. Jakubec said it was Bela's secret room and she had been ordered to stay out of it.

Inside the room were many books relating to poisons and preservatives. There were plans and methods of strangulation, and notes on how to drain blood from a human body. They also found letters between Bela and over 70 women he had been soliciting.

Some of the women were later identified as those in the metal drums. After the search of the house and grounds had been carried out, 24 intact human bodies had been discovered.

Vampire of Cinkota.

Some of the bodies were found buried around the property but despite not being in a barrel, they had been embalmed in methanol. Almost all of the victims still had their features so Charles and his team set to work identifying them, which they mostly managed to do.

The investigation contacted all the local police departments where the victims had lived, to get more details on each of their disappearances. No letters had been written to the women but a search of the local newspapers yielded results.

Not only had Bela been placing advertisements in newspapers, but he had also been corresponding with his victims through the matrimonial columns, right under the nose of everyone reading. Due to their fear of being caught out with a fortune teller, the women had responded using the classifieds.

This method of communication allowed Bela to find perfect victims, those who wouldn't be missed. When autopsies of the bodies were carried out, more disturbing facts came to light. One of the victim's was Bela's second wife, who he claimed had run off with a younger man.

The truth was that Bela had killed them both, and the younger man was buried beside his second wife in the grounds of the house. Almost all of his victims had been strangled to death with his bare hands or a section of rope.

Some of the bodies exhibited puncture wounds on the neck caused by someone biting into it. Most of the bodies had been drained of blood before being preserved. When word got around of the bitemarks on the necks, the Vampire of Cinkota was born.

On the run.

Due to the teeth puncture marks, Charles concluded that Bela had most likely been practicing vampirism. His routine of working at night and luring gullible women to his home certainly reeked of a bloodsucker.

In the Autumn of 1916, with the story making the national – and international – press, Charles received a letter from a military doctor. He claimed that Bela Kiss had been injured in the war and was recuperating at a Serbian hospital.

Charles and a team immediately travelled to Serbia, which was then under Hungarian control. They arrived in the middle of the night so as not to scare off Bela. But when they arrived on the ward, they were in for a shock.

Somehow, Bela was already on to them and had substituted his body with an injured soldier from the same ward. The hospital went into lockdown but Bela had already escaped into the night, never to be seen again.

The next day, Charles went to the press and told the public that the Vampire of Cinkota was alive and on the run. He warned the Hungarian people not to approach him as he was considered an extremely dangerous person.

Soon enough, Bela and his 24 victims fell into legend – but then the sightings began.

Kiss of the vampire.

When Charles went public, the police received reports of Bela sightings across the country. As the country was still war-torn, the ability to follow every lead became impossible and the case eventually fell into the realm of the cold.

In 1919, a shopkeeper in Budapest reported seeing Bela walking along a nearby street towards a church but police found no trace of him. In 1920, a member of the French Foreign Legion went to a Budapest police station with an unusual story.

He claimed that Bela had joined the legion under the name of Hoffman. Charles was made aware of the report and noted that Bela had used the name of Hoffman in some of the letters to his victims. When his team followed up the report, Hoffman had mysteriously deserted the legion without warning.

In New York City in 1932, a homicide detective who was aware of the Hungarian case claimed to have seen Bela at the exit of the New York City Subway in Times Square. He followed the man only to lose him in the crowds.

Many more sightings came in from across the world but by that point, Bela Kiss had become a myth. What is known is that he killed at least 24 people, drank their blood and preserved most of their bodies in metal drums. What we don't know is whether he continued to kill. Though no further victims were attributed to him, there were suggestions he may have got cleverer at disposing of the bodies.

Whatever happened to the Vampire of Cinkota, there is a very slim supernatural possibility that he remains in the shadows, drinking the blood of unreported victims. Sometimes known as the kiss of the vampire.

THE SCOTTISH VAMPIRE

A Scottish man obsessed with the occult, sacrificed his friend, ate parts of head and drank his blood from a cup, in an effort to become a vampire and gain immortality.

In the late 1990s and early 2000s there was a rise in vampire entertainment. The movie industry was seeing a resurgence in vampire films, previously popular in the 1960s and 1970s. These included films like Underworld, Blade, and Queen of the Damned, among many others.

Vampire video games were on the rise as were books and websites dedicated to the subculture. Referred to as the cult of vampirism, it had its roots in power and dominance, in which blood gave a person energy and immortality.

Vampires are often associated with outcasts making them easily relatable to many teenagers and adults. However, there is a clear line between enjoying vampire culture and committing a brutal ritualistic murder in order to achieve immortal life.

Which is exactly what happened in the case of Allan Menzies, who on 20th January 2003 killed his friend, ate parts of his head and drank his blood from a cup. He had been directly influenced by the film Queen of the Damned, which he had seen over 100 times.

He claimed one of the vampires from the movie convinced him to kill his friend and drink his blood in order to become a vampire and achieve that much sought after immortality. But as it turned out, Allan had been on the path to murder for quite some time.

Under the radar.

Born 21st April 1981 in Edinburgh, Allan was withdrawn from an early age. He struggled to make friends and hardly ever wanted to play. During his school years, he spent most of his time in his bedroom rocking back and forth making unusual noises.

He kept his curtains closed and kept himself to himself. His hobbies were watching movies, reading books, and playing games, most of which were horror-based with a vampiric edge. Allan suffered from panic attacks when faced with change.

It was clear when psychiatrists looked back on his life that he was suffering from schizophrenia, which was later diagnosed at his trial. In the 1990s, mental health was not quite the open book it is today which meant many sufferers went under the radar. Allan was one of those.

Despite his lack of social interaction, he was considered a kind young boy who kept his room tidy and completed chores with no troubles. But as he turned from a boy to a teenager, his parents began to see worrying changes in him.

At the age of 13, Allan had deliberately overdosed on paracetamol at least five times, three of which required hospital treatment. Still, he wasn't properly seen by mental health professionals. At the age of 14, he got into trouble at school for disruption and was given detention, where he stabbed another boy in the stomach with a nine-inch hunting knife.

The turning point.

Following a trial in a juvenile court in Edinburgh in 1996, he was convicted of assault resulting in severe injury and ordered to be detained for three years. The sentence was served at St. Mary's Kenmure, in Glasgow, a secure unit for the rehabilitation of young people referred from the courts.

While a resident at the site, he attempted to take his own life by using his pyjamas as a ligature, tied to a bedpost. In 1999, he was released and returned to live with his parents but they divorced soon after he returned.

Allan Menzies, the Scottish Vampire being transferred from court.

Splitting his time between two homes affected Allan further and he began to self-harm again, this time with blades. His mother recalled an incident when he was twenty. Allan walked into the kitchen with his arm covered in blood, the result of a cutting. He could not explain why he had a cut on his arm.

In 2001, Allan attempted suicide again which resulted in another hospitalisation. His mother told doctors there was something wrong with him and sought help but no help was forthcoming at the time. Allan spent most of his time at his father's home following the suicide attempt.

His father claimed he was mostly interested in computers, films, and bizarrely – ferrets. It was later discovered that Allan would head out into the countryside and hunt small animals to kill with his bare hands. A pupil at his school later confirmed he had killed a cat on school grounds but wasn't held to account.

Then, in August 2002, the movie Queen of the Damned was released on DVD and VHS in the UK, a film that had hit cinemas a few months earlier. Allan became fascinated with the story of the Vampire Lestat played by Stuart Townsend, and Akasha played by Aaliyah in her last film.

For Allan, he had found the Holy Grail.

Akasha came to life.

Everything about his life began to make sense to him. The social exclusion, the violence, the distaste of daylight and normal people. He became so fascinated with the film and its lore that he consumed vampire novels by Anne Rice, the creator of Queen of the Damned, along with other vampire literature.

He came to believe he was a vampire, more so when the delusions kicked in. He watched the Queen of the Damned over a hundred times in just a few months, sometimes replaying it multiple times in a day. He hallucinated that the character of Akasha came to life and spoke to him directly.

She told him to kill another human being and drink their blood to became a vampire just like her but Allan didn't have a victim lined up. Until December when one of his distant friends, 21-year-old Thomas McKendrick came over to watch the film.

Thomas voiced his distaste for the film and they argued over it. Allan didn't like the fact Thomas was insulting not only the film, but the vampire who spoke to him. It was then he realised he had found the perfect victim.

He stabbed Thomas 42 times in the chest and stomach before smashing his skull open with ten blows from a heavy hammer. Allan ripped pieces of Thomas's head off and chewed on them, swallowing some of it, but he realised he needed to drink the blood.

He rolled the body onto its side so he could collect the blood in a small cup to drink. After collecting as much blood as he could, he resorted to pushing the cup into an open wound to fill it, then continued drinking, spurred on by the belief he was about to become a fully-fledged vampire.

The woodland where the shallow grave with Thomas's body was found.

Buried in the woods.

Later that night, he placed Thomas's remains into a wheelie bin and rolled it to a nearby wood where he buried the body in a shallow grave. Thomas was reported as missing by his mother, who bumped into Allan while in a supermarket.

Allan asked her if she knew how to remove bloodstains. Disturbed, she walked away and tried to brush it from her memory. Three weeks after her son disappeared, the comment of the bloodstains made perfect sense.

Police were alerted to the gravesite when a dog started digging at it. There, they uncovered Thomas's body. Allan was arrested within hours due to Thomas last being seen with him and the statement from Thomas's mother.

Three psychiatrists diagnosed Allan as a psychopath suffering from anti-social personality disorder and paranoid schizophrenia. They were shocked he had even been allowed out in public let alone never being diagnosed with the disorder.

His lawyers made a plea of guilty to culpable homicide by reason of diminished responsibility. The Crown refused the plea and ordered Allan to stand trial where he was found guilty of murder. While waiting for sentencing, he was transferred to Carstairs State Hospital in South Lanarkshire.

'I got his soul.'

Carstairs is a high-security psychiatric hospital, home to around 140 high-risk patients requiring mental health care. On 8th October 2003, Allan was sentenced to life in prison with a minimum term of 18 years.

Instead of being returned to Carstairs, he was sent to HM Prison Edinburgh, a general population facility sometimes known as Saughton Prison from the old name for the general area. There, he was assessed as being a suicide risk and placed under close observation.

In November, he was suddenly considered low risk and moved to a different prison, the maximum security HM Prison Shotts in North Lanarkshire. A year later on 16th November 2004, Allan killed himself by using a sheet as a ligature.

After his death, newly released court reports unveiled some of the words spoken by Allan. In relation to a possible sentence, he said, '*I'm going to do 20 to 25 [years] for this, for doing him with a hammer and a knife. But I don't care because I got his soul.*'

When describing the murder, he was matter-of-fact about it. '*I pushed the knife through his throat and into his brain. I drank his blood and ate a bit of his head. There was blood everywhere and I buried him up in the woods.*'

Directly after the murder, he wrote a note on a page from an Anne Rice book. It read, '*the blood is the life, I have drunk the blood and it shall be mine, for I have seen the horror.*' In Allan's head, he had become the vampire he wanted to be. To others, he was a grotesque killer who could have been stopped earlier.

"The world changes,
WE DO NOT, THEREIN LIES
THE IRONY THAT KILLS US."

- Anne Rice

THE LESBIAN VAMPIRE KILLER

A lesbian lover of all things occult claimed to survive off the blood of animals before convincing her friends she was a vampire who needed to kill to satisfy her craving for the red stuff.

Multiple personality disorders have been given the horror entertainment treatment so many times it has become synonymous with having literal different personalities. Though there are similarities, it is an often misunderstood disorder.

Today, the condition is known as dissociative identity disorder (DID) and is defined by the presence of one or more alternate personalities, known as alters. It is characterised by identity fragmentation and not an army of different people living in the same body.

Which is why when an Australian murderer was diagnosed as having four to six different personalities, it was met with much scepticism. But for some researchers, it was proof that multiple personalities living in the same body was possible.

The murderer's name was Tracey Avril Wigginton, who on 20th October 1989, stabbed to death 47-year-old council worker Edward Baldock. She then partially severed his head and drank blood directly from his exposed neck.

The murder itself was as horrific as it was vampiric in nature, spurred on by her belief that she needed human blood to survive, to get stronger. A psychiatrist later conclude Wigginton had at least four personalities. On the night of the murder, it was a personality named April who came to the fore, named after her violent adoptive mother.

Tracey Wigginton, the Lesbian Vampire Killer.

A dark path.

Wigginton was born in 1965 in Rockhampton, north Australia. At the age of three she was adopted by her grandparents following her parents' divorce. Her mother did not have the means or mental capability to look after her anymore.

Her grandparents were known to be abusive towards her and it was claimed she was sexually, physically, and emotionally abused. In her early teens, she began to gain weight and came out as a bisexual.

When she was 15, after her grandfather died, she attacked a man who had come to visit her grandmother. She fractured his nose and slashed his fingers with a kitchen knife, before violently pushing his hearing aid into his ear canal.

Her grandmother died in 1981 when she was 16 and she moved back in with her mother, only to find her mother did not accept her sexual preferences. When she received a $300,000 pay-out from her grandparents will, she moved in with a friend, and for a while, everything was going smoothly.

She was known as a loving human, gifted with the creativity of art, and attended the local church having become a devout Catholic. She met a young man and became pregnant by him but weeks into the pregnancy, she miscarried.

It led her down a dark path and she refused to attend mass at the church, in time blaming god for her lot in life. She came out as gay before venturing into the world of the occult. Before long, she had a craving for blood.

A domineering presence.

During her late teens and early twenties, Wigginton began to go deep into the occult, believing she was a vampire. To placate her vampiric desires, she visited the local butcher who supplied her with pigs and cows blood.

She allegedly warmed it up in a microwave and drank it from a cup. Other times, she lured local pets to her home before killing them and drinking their warm blood. She was also alleged to have killed a wild animal with a hunting knife and scooped the blood from the wound into her mouth.

Only months before the murder, she got into a relationship with Lisa Ptaschinski, a local woman one year her senior. To placate her new partner's desire for blood, Lisa would cut her arms and neck so Wigginton could slurp the blood from her open wound.

Two more friends, a lesbian couple named Kim Jervis and Tracy Waugh, were brought into her world of the occult and vampirism. Due to her large size, Wigginton was a domineering presence who convinced her girlfriend and the couple she had supernatural powers.

All three believed Wigginton was a vampire who could even make herself disappear. In the weeks before the murder, the four of them had a midnight picnic at a nearby cemetery, which resulted in them removing a headstone and taking it back to Wigginton's home.

The headstone took pride of place in the living room and gave Wigginton the impetus she needed to convince her friends further. She made them watch a notorious video nasty that showed real people being executed and told them she had been thinking of killing someone for their blood.

L'Amours.

The night before the murder, Wigginton dyed her hair jet black and told her friends she needed to feed on a victim's blood, or she wouldn't be able to maintain her sanity, as much as it was.

They went out to a lesbian nightclub in Brisbane's Fortitude Valley called L'Amours. There, before the club was overrun with partygoers, Wigginton convinced them they needed to claim a victim for her to feed on. Together, they came up with a plan.

At 11.30pm, they left L'Amours and set off in Wigginton's car, to cruise the streets, looking for a man around the time the pubs kicked people out. At midnight, they spotted 47-year-old Edward Baldock staggering out from the Caledonia Club and followed him.

When he was alone, Wigginton pulled up beside him and lured him into the car with the offer of a good time. The drunk father of four went for the forbidden fruit and gave into temptation, falling into the back seat, ready for some fun.

Wigginton drove four miles away to Orleigh Park, an isolated area on the river in the West End, a place she knew would be deserted at that time of night. She parked up and took Edward with her into the darkness of the park, leaving the other three in the car.

Wigginton removed her top and told Edward to get himself ready as she went to relieve herself. But she went back to the car, grabbed the knife she had been sharpening for days, and told Lisa to come with her to watch.

Brutal murder.

Edward had stripped off and folded all his clothes into a neat pile when Wigginton walked up to him from the darkness and plunged the long knife into his neck. She then stabbed him another 27 times in the back and neck.

As his body fell to the ground, she ordered Lisa to go back to the car, as she got to work partially severing Edward's head. As he lay dying, she leaned in and drank the blood from the large open wound, savouring every drop she could.

After, she sat down next to the body and smoked a cigarette, later claiming to have '*felt nothing.*' Upon return to the car, Lisa and the other two could smell the blood on her breath. At 5am the next morning, a jogger stumbled upon Edward's body which had been left in the open.

Though Wigginton thought they had planned the perfect murder, they hadn't. Next to the body, police found a pair of shoes containing Wigginton's bank card, with her name on full display. She only realised she had left it the next morning.

She drove back to Orleigh Park to discover police had swarmed the area. She said to one of the friend's, '*oh my god, it's real.*' It was one of the instances in which she was thought to have had a personality disorder, as they are often categorised by amnesia and a sense of feeling detached.

The police arrested Wigginton and the other three less than two hours later, and within hours, they had confessed the truth of what had gone down. It was then that psychiatrists decided to assess Wigginton further – and some scary revelations came to light.

The power of god.

Wigginton agreed to be hypnotised. When she went under, she responded to questions using different voices and mannerisms. The main personality was Big Tracey, who was thought to be the dominant personality and an amalgamation of all of them.

Another was Bobby, a violent 16-year-old who hated the world. Little Tracey was a scared child but April was the one that terrified assessors. April was named after her abusive grandmother and would speak in a lower voice, claiming she needed blood to survive.

However, one assessor believed Wigginton was making the whole thing up and suggested she hadn't been hypnotised at all. She showed no remorse for the murder. The only thing she was sorry about was that she had been caught.

After being cleared fit for the courts, she and the other three went on trial for murder, with Wigginton the only one pleading guilty. She blamed the murder on her desire for blood and that it released a repressed rage from a childhood filled with abuse.

She said, *'it's scary to have that much power. It's playing god with life and death. Nobody should have that sort of power but we all do.'* Lisa and the other lesbian couple had become so convinced in Wigginton's powers they truly believed she was a vampire.

Lesbian vampire killer.

In 1991, Wigginton was sentenced to life in prison for murder. Lisa was also sentenced to life after a lengthy trial deemed her culpable in the murder. Kim Jervis got 18 years for manslaughter, later reduced to 12, and Tracey Waugh was acquitted for her part in the crime.

They all claimed the sole reason for the murder was to enable Wigginton to feed from another human. In 2006, Wigginton attacked a fellow inmate and prison guard during a row but was not brought to trial for it.

In 2008, 17 years later, Lisa was released under a resettlement program with a new identity. In 2012, after 21 years in prison, and much to the anger of the Australian public, the lesbian vampire killer, Tracey Wigginton was released on parole.

The release brought widespread criticism of the courts. A detective involved in the original case, said the murder was the most brutal and disturbing he had ever worked on. Edward's family were understandably completely against her release.

Despite the anger surrounding the release, Wigginton kept herself to herself afterwards. Until seven years later, in 2019, when she roared back into the news. After accessing a Facebook account under the name of one of her 'personalities', she posted the following two images.

After, she shared more photos of vampires, skeletons and real human remains. Despite calls for a return to prison, the parole board decided she had not violated her release conditions but confirmed she would remain under supervision for the rest of her life.

Which was of little relief to Edward's family and the lives of those she managed to control and ruin. The lesbian vampire killer roams Australia today as a free woman, whose actions after her release prove there is no remorse, and that April may be simmering beneath the surface.

THE VAMPIRE RAPIST

A serial killer and government contractor, claiming to be a vampire, was exposed when a victim escaped his home – where she had been raped and drained of blood.

Sometimes, the persona people show to the world hides a dark version of themselves. John Brennan Crutchley appeared to be living a perfect life, the American dream. He was a maths genius with a high IQ and held a high-security position with the government where he oversaw projects for NASA.

But beneath the surface, he was a dark vampiric individual who was suspected to have killed around 30 people. He was ultimately caught when he kidnapped a teenage victim, subjected her to hours of rape and torture, and drained her blood to the point of death. Blood that he needed to drink to survive.

Going back to his childhood, we begin to see the first signs of the monster awakening. Born on 1st October 1946 in Clarksburg, West Virginia, Crutchley did not have an easy childhood. Shortly before his birth, his older sister died during surgery and their mother hoped to have another daughter to replace her.

Instead, she was gifted a son but hated him the moment he was born. Though disappointed with his sex, she believed she could turn him into a girl, and made him dress up in girl's clothing until the age of seven when schoolteachers began noticing a withdrawn young boy.

He didn't have many friends and began playing with electronic gadgets in the basement of the family home. It became not only a hobby but something that grew into a career. By the time he left school, he was earning money rebuilding complex radio systems for local people.

He hid his dark side well.

When he was 24, he graduated with a bachelor's degree in physics from a private college in Ohio and went on to get a master's degree in engineering from a university in Washington D.C. He had married shortly before getting his bachelor's degree but the relationship ended when his wife left him.

He moved to Indiana and got work at the Delco Electronics Corporation before finding his way into the General Motor's company. In the mid-seventies, he remarried and had a son with his new wife. He worked around Washington D.C. at various tech companies before moving his family to Florida in 1983 to work at the Harris Corporation, a government defence contractor.

To his colleagues, he was a generous, hard-working family man who lived a lavish lifestyle tinted with big career successes. But little did they know, he had a dark side that he hid well from the world, almost as well as Ted Bundy did. His true self would not be discovered until 1985.

It was Thanksgiving 1985, on November 21st, when his wife and young son decided to leave Florida to visit family in Maryland. The then 39-year-old Crutchley had the house to himself which afforded him the opportunity he had been waiting for.

He drove around Brevard County in Florida seeking out a victim and he didn't have to wait long. He picked up a 19-year-old hitchhiker from California who was visiting friends in the nearby city of Melbourne. It was probably the biggest mistake of her life.

Draining the hitchhiker.

Instead of taking her to where she wanted to go, Crutchley drove her to his home saying he needed to pick up a notebook as he was on his way to work. Instead of going inside to collect a notebook, he wrapped a cord around her neck, choked her unconscious and dragged her body up the driveway into the house.

After removing all of her clothing, he tied her to the island worktop in his kitchen. She awoke to a scene out of a horror film. On the worktop next to her, Crutchley had set up a video camera – to record everything he was about to do.

After raping her multiple times, he inserted syringes into her veins and began drawing blood. Once he was certain the blood was clean, he squirted it into a glass and began drinking it. As he drank it, he told her that he was a vampire and that he needed her blood to survive.

When she was too weak to fight back, he untied her and placed her in the bathtub, washing off her body for the next round of horror. He returned an hour later and sexually assaulted her for an extended period of time before once again drawing blood from her using the needles.

As she weakened further, he left her in the bathtub for the entire night in the knowledge she couldn't escape due to the lack of blood. In the morning, he raped her again and drew more blood from her, almost to the point of death.

For around 18 hours, Crutchley had alternated between raping her and draining her blood so he could drink it. He then handcuffed her to the bathtub. He told her if she tried to escape he would return to cut her throat.

Lost 45% of her blood.

By the late afternoon, the girl had built up enough strength and courage to escape the bathroom. She stumbled out the house only to collapse due to the weakness. Somehow, she managed to crawl to a busy road.

As it was getting dark, many motorists didn't notice the nude handcuffed teenager covered in blood. But soon enough, a car pulled over and a man went to help her. She screamed at him to not take her back to that house.

An ambulance arrived shortly after to rush her to hospital, followed by the police. Doctors were shocked to find that she was close to death and had lost approximately 45% of her blood. Had she not escaped the house then one more round of bloodletting would have killed her.

They also confirmed she would have died within ten hours if she had not been given medical attention. For a while, she was too traumatised to tell the police what happened but when she did, they swarmed Crutchley's house at 2.30am and arrested him for kidnapping and violent assault.

They found enough evidence inside the house to corroborate the girl's story including the syringes and bloodstained bathtub. The videotape in the camera had been partially erased which would have shown the horrific rape and bloodletting. The vampire was taken into custody – and then, things got really disturbing.

Many more victims.

When police searched the house, they found the teenager's ID in a stash of other ID's belonging to multiple women. Hidden in a drawer, they found several locks of hair and jewellery not belonging to his wife.

Immediately, police suspected they were trophies from other victims. Following the house search, they ransacked his work office where they stumbled upon a stash of photos with various women in sexually explicit poses, all of whom had been restrained and gagged. Two of the images showed Crutchley with his hands around the women's necks.

A second search of his home turned up a box of index cards. Written on the cards were the names of people he'd had sex with, either from previous relationships or from casual sexual encounters. On the cards, he listed their names, graded them on their sexual performance, and noted down various sexual 'abilities' they were deemed good for.

Police tracked down some of the women but could not trace the others, suspecting Crutchley had used false names on some occasions. Of the women they tracked down, they told police Crutchley could turn violent during sex and cross the line into sexual assault.

But there was one woman named on a card who caught the attention of the police. Deborah Fitzjohn was one of Crutchley's former girlfriends who disappeared in 1978 after they had lived together briefly in Washington D.C.

A few months later, her nude body was found in an isolated wood. Due to the decomposition, there was not evidence to charge Crutchley with a crime but police suspected at the time he was responsible. In fact, when they looked at his movements over the past decade, a disturbing pattern emerged.

'Simply a kinky guy.'

Another ID card belonged to a female hitchhiker who had gone missing earlier in 1985. She had vanished without a trace but the ID card linked Crutchley to her disappearance. Police later uncovered various human bones surrounding the house where he lived.

The problem was that the evidence was only circumstantial, though in today's world, advancements in forensic technology would have seen him convicted on them. As it was, the only crime they could charge him with was the kidnapping, rape, and bodily harm of the teenager who escaped.

In June 1986, he struck a plea deal to go guilty on the kidnapping and rape in order to have the bodily harm charge removed. That charge was entirely linked with the removal of blood. During the trial, Crutchley admitted he had been introduced to bloodletting by an unidentified woman in 1970.

Since then, he believed he needed blood to survive, going as far as believing he was a vampire. He couldn't name the woman but suspected she was a vampire too. Oddly, his wife told reporters that the kidnapping wasn't that serious and that Critchley was simply a kinky guy.

He was sentenced to 25 years to life in prison with 50 subsequent years of parole. Which is why when he was released only ten years later in 1996, the police became concerned. They were still certain Crutchley was a serial killer, claiming lives to satisfy his vampiric bloodlust.

Serial killer in the shadows.

Police followed him everywhere, and only one day after his release, Critchley was caught smoking marijuana which was an instant parole violation. Despite him saying it was to ease his anxiety regarding his release from prison, the violation resulted in a life sentence.

Six years later, on 30th March 2002, Crutchley killed himself in his prison cell by placing a plastic bag over his head. An enquiry confirmed he had died as a result of erotic asphyxiation, an intentional practice of restricting oxygen to the brain for the purposes of sexual arousal.

New investigators reopened the Crutchley case to see if they could find more details of possible murders. As they backtracked his movements and corresponded the ID cards along with missing persons reports, they discovered something horrifying.

He was positively linked with 12 females who had either disappeared or were murdered. Including the disappearance of two teenage girls from Maryland in 1975 and a rape-murder from the same area the following year. He was also linked to the murders of two U.S. Navy women in Virginia.

The same investigation claimed it was possible Crutchley had claimed more than 30 victims. But due to the lack of evidence at the time and his premature death, he was never convicted of a single murder, which means a lot of the cases of missing and murdered women remain open and unsolved.

What is clear is that John Crutchley was able to hide his vampiric nature from the world until he was caught out by a teenage victim who found the strength to escape. If it wasn't for her, the vampire rapist could have claimed many more victims.

"Listen to them,
CHILDREN OF THE NIGHT.
WHAT MUSIC THEY MAKE."

BONUS: BIZARRE TRUE CRIME PREVIEW

The Bizarre True Crime books are a bestselling non-fiction anthology series from Ben Oakley and Twelvetrees Camden. Here's a sample story, one of twenty, from Volume 10 of the series.

MYSTERIOUS DEATHS OF TWO JUNGLE HIKERS

Two Dutch girls died while hiking through a Panamanian jungle, in a weird case that includes body parts, unusual photos, bleached bones, and an unnerving sense that something was terribly wrong.

The great outdoors tempts hikers and adventurers seeking to discover the immense beauty of the planet gifted to us. The wilderness is more than a place to wander, it represents freedom, peace, and the ability to do what humans do best; explore.

Thus, it is with such heart-breaking hindsight that the wilderness has claimed many lives. From mountains, icescapes, deserts, swamps, and jungles, many humans have simply vanished into thin air or met their end. Some by accident, some not.

When friends, 21-year-old Kris Kremers and 22-year-old Lisanne Froon, left the Netherlands to go backpacking through Panama, they expected nothing less than a life-changing experience. The plan was to use their six-week break to learn more about themselves and the world.

Both women planned to learn Spanish and volunteer with local children's groups. They wanted to do something of significance for the local community, something to be remembered. Instead, their story became one of danger, and a mystery yet to be solved.

Welcome to the jungle.

Having saved for six months, Kris and Lisanne arrived in Panama on 15th March 2014. They travelled around the Central American country for two weeks before arriving in Boquete, in the province of Chiriquí, a mountain town and gateway to the great jungles.

They planned to stay with a local family for one month, using it as a base to explore the area and do volunteer work for children in the community. On 1st April 2014, both women accessed their Facebook profiles and let their friends and families know they would be exploring the clouded forests around the giant active Baru Volcano (Volcán Barú).

Selfie of Kris Kremers and Lisanne Froon taken during the fateful hike.

Baru is the tallest mountain in Panama, at 11,398 ft (3,474 metres), and the twelfth tallest in Central America. It holds a unique position that if you were to climb it on a clear day, you could see the Pacific Ocean on one side and the Caribbean Sea on the other.

Before they went off into the jungle surrounding the volcano, they were spotted having an early lunch with two Dutch men, who have never been identified. One of the dogs from a local restaurant followed the girls into the jungle at around 11am, as it had a habit of accompanying hikers in the region.

On the night of 1st April, the dog returned to its owners without Kris and Lisanne. It was then the owners realised something bad may have happened. The family the women were staying with confirmed they had not returned to the residence.

Back in the Netherlands, Kris and Lisanne's parents stopped receiving text messages from them. Both women had promised to text every single day without fail. Due to the location, it was a possibility they had simply lost signal, gone deeper into the jungle, and had made their way back in the middle of the night.

But on the morning of the 2nd when they missed their connection with a local mountain guide, it became evident something had gone terribly wrong.

Discovery of backpack.

The Panamanian police did what they could but were limited in their capacity to explore the jungle looking for two hikers. As word reached the Netherlands, the case blew up and became a huge story in the Dutch press.

Five days after the disappearance, on 6th April, the women's parents landed in Panama, flanked by Dutch detectives and officials. The search began the same day. A large team of local police, Dutch investigators, dog units, and mountain rescue flooded the jungle around the town.

For the next ten days, the search party pushed through areas of jungle rarely hiked, even to the peak of the Baru Volcano. They found nothing, no trace of the women, no clues, and no idea what had happened to them. The jungle had consumed them. The search was called off.

Over two months later, on 14th June, a local woman discovered a backpack in a rice paddy along the banks of the river leading out of Boquete, many miles from where the women had entered the jungle.

The backpack belonged to Lisanne. It contained sunglasses, a small amount of cash in American Dollars, her passport, water bottle, her camera, their underwear, and both their phones. Despite the location of the backpack, the items inside were in near-perfect condition.

Which is where the case took a turn to the dark side.

One of the photos retrieved from the camera, taken seven days after they entered the jungle.

Disturbing call logs and photos.

An investigation into the phones and the camera revealed some disturbing information. Six hours after the girls had entered the jungle, someone dialled 112 and 911, the emergency numbers in the Netherlands and Panama respectively.

On 4th April, three days after they entered the jungle, Kris's phone battery died. Lisanne's iPhone was turned on and off for another day in an attempt to make a connection. She had dialled the emergency number 77 times before 5th April when no more calls were made.

However, the phone's history didn't end there. Between the 5th and 11th April, the iPhone was turned on and off multiple times but the phone was not accessed. It meant either the wrong pin code had been entered or no pin code had been entered. A detailed investigation of the phone showed the wrong pin code had been entered on some of those occasions.

If the phone logs were disturbing enough, the photos were on a whole other level. The first photos were taken on the morning of 1st April and showed the women on a trail near the Continental Divide. Also known as the Great Divide, it separates most of the Americas with its high mountainous regions.

Nothing seemed untoward until the second set of photos were revealed. On 8th April, seven days after the disappearance, over 90 photos showed their belongings spread out over rocks, bags, and sweet wrappers. They appeared to be in deep jungle in the middle of the night.

Other photos taken with the flash showed mounds of dirt, a backpack strap, and a mirror on a rock. The most disturbing was a photo of the back of

Kris's head. Some sleuths believe they can see blood on the top of her head but it's not clear enough to prove. There are no photos of the women's faces or other body parts.

While searching the area where the backpack had been found, police found Kris's clothes perfectly folded on the edge of the river. Then, two months later, body parts were discovered.

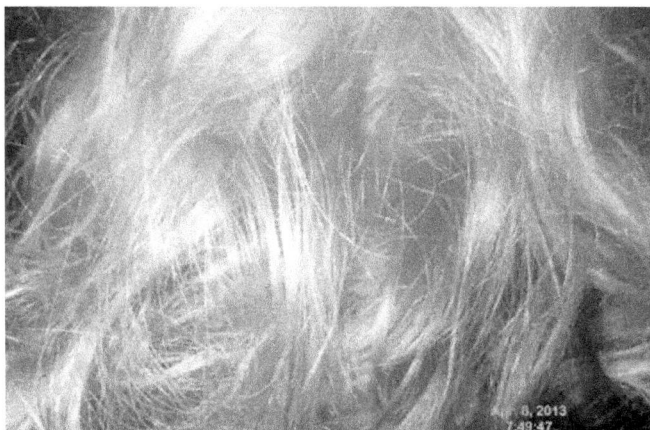

Chilling photo of the top of Kris's head, taken seven days after they disappeared.

Discovery of bones.

Two months after the discovery of the backpack, Lisanne's boot was found, with her decomposed foot still inside. Soon after, the rest of her bones turned up, still with decomposing pieces of flesh hanging off them.

A pelvic bone was discovered near the boot, belonging to Kris. A few miles away, the remainder of her bones were found, spread over a wide area. Unlike Lisanne's remains, it appeared Kris's bones had been bleached clean. They were perfectly white.

DNA testing confirmed the remains belonged to both women. Panamanian police interviewed hundreds of local residents and looked for more clues but came no closer to the truth of what had happened to the two hikers.

The forensic examination of the bones confirmed there were no scratches on any of them, neither natural nor purposeful. Due to the decomposition, it was concluded there was not enough evidence to determine a cause of death. So, what really happened out there in the jungle?

Could Kris and Lisanne have succumbed to an unfortunate accident, or was there something more nefarious involved? Did they become more adventurous the longer they walked, or did they lose their way, unable to find their way back?

Logical explanation.

The trail itself is relatively well laid out, leading some researchers to believe it would be impossible to get lost. However, it's not uncommon for hikers to go off the beaten-track or become adventurous along the way. Hell, I got lost in Regent's Park once, and I live right next door!

But this is where things get more curious. The area they were hiking was close to a river, multiple villages, and near the Continental Divide, a trail easy to follow. If they got lost on the first night, it's possible they could still have found their way out the following morning.

The fact the phone logs showed the emergency number being dialled 77 times for the next four days, meant the girls may have been trapped. But by accident or with intent? The most logical explanation, and one put forward by Dutch researchers, suggests the two women had got lost and then become stuck due to known flash flooding in the area that time of year.

Flash flooding suggests the women may have drowned or become injured and unable to walk out. Being injured would explain why they couldn't escape the jungle. Drowning is an unusual one because both phones were working in the days after the disappearance, with Lisanne's iPhone being turned on and off for ten days after.

It's unlikely someone would have survived ten days in the jungle with no survival experience but it has happened before. As the result of an accident, did Kris survive longer than Lisanne? Or was Kris on the run through the jungle from someone or something?

The TripAdvisor conundrum.

There is another side of this story. Many are split 50/50 on whether the pair died in a tragic accident or were victims of a violent crime. The more we dive into the case, the more bizarre it becomes. The more questions we ask, the less answers we have.

The women only set off on a small hike, as they were due to meet a guide the following morning for a longer trek. When the story broke around the world, some Northern European female travellers spoke of their concern and fear of some of the hiking guides in the area.

Some have posted reviews to TripAdvisor warning people of one of the local male guides. The first one is from a Dutch female travelling solo, who used a guide from the same area. The review was posted in May 2022.

'He was super friendly, helped me, held my hand during the climbs on the pianista trail. Until I realized that help was only there for me, not for my 3 fellow travellers. In the days that followed, I was besieged by messages, invitations.'

'During a horse ride and a trip to hot springs, he suddenly turned out to be our driver (while he had nothing to do with horse riding) and he got into the hot spring. Not exactly what you expect from a taxi driver.'

'I didn't feel comfortable in his surroundings and was very happy that my fellow travellers had accompanied me so that I was not alone with him, which was what he meant. In the 3 days I was in Boquete, I got constant messages asking to come to his home. I have my doubts about his intentions. As a European woman, don't go alone.'

Another, posted in 2019, was even more damning.

'It took me almost a year to finally post this review. I strongly recommend women to not hire Feliciano as your guide if you're by yourself.'

'Not long after we left he subtly started to flirt with me and also touching me, first my hand, but also my arms, shoulder and legs, even after telling him many times to stop doing that.'

'He wears a big machete and suggested to chop off my legs. He has an obsession for Northern European women and I felt very unsafe.'

Sexual harassment does not a killer make. However, there are many other stories about guides and locals in the area, who had at one time or another left tourists feeling scared for their lives. Mostly Northern European female tourists.

Yet, both reviews were posted many years after Kris and Lisanne's deaths. It's possible a narrative was building against the guide as a possible suspect. The guide in question lives in a cabin with his son a few miles from where the bones were found, yet there is no solid evidence to confirm his involvement.

If there were reviews about his harassment before the event, then they would have been more damning. As such, and as it would be in a court of law, they are inadmissible. Scary and worrying but inadmissible, nonetheless.

Things could have gone wrong quickly.

Panama is mostly safe for tourists, the country thrives on the industry. But there are many towns and cities in Central and South American countries which are considered dangerous. Boquete is a small town with a main street and a number of side roads.

Venture into the bad part of town and you'll find drug dealers and groups of people playing gangsters. Some visitors to the town after the bodies were found, were convinced the two women were murdered, but the residents seemed to be silent about what really happened.

It's a possibility the girls may have stumbled upon something they shouldn't have. If they came across drug dealers or wannabe gangsters, things could have gone wrong quickly. Lisanne's father returned to Boquete for a candlelit vigil and became involved in the story. He became convinced a local taxi driver had followed them into the jungle and murdered them.

The same taxi driver died mysteriously in a drowning accident not long after. As his death was seen as accidental, an autopsy was not carried out. Some believe he was murdered to hide the truth.

In recent years, theories of cannibal natives and human traffickers have been spread around. There is no evidence for cannibals in the region. Human traffickers are known to operate in Panama, but the fact the pair's bones were found suggests they were not abducted into the slave trade.

One final spanner in the works.

When I put on my Agatha Christie hat and turn on web-sleuthing mode, I come to two possible conclusions. One, the pair suffered an accident, got lost, and died from delirium in the woods. Two, they were attacked by someone or a group living in one of the nearby towns.

If there had been no phone logs or photos, then the narrative of two women going into a jungle alone and succumbing to accidental deaths would seem logical. But there were phone logs confirming one of the phones was checking for a signal ten days later. And there were photos.

But if a killer was in the jungle with them that day, why did he not destroy the phones? Why take photos in the middle of the night, seven days after the women disappeared? Why not destroy the backpack?

The most unusual clue to come out of the jungle is the photo of the top of Kris's head, taken with a flash in the middle of the night, seven days after they entered the jungle. Had Kris succumbed to delirium and delusion? Because of her state of mind, maybe she thought she had heard or seen something in the jungle and was using the flash to deter the danger.

If Kris had survived seven days in the jungle, rather than taking weird pictures of the ground and darkness, she might have known she was going to die. In those cases, a person might take a photo of their face or a message for their family back home. But the closest to a personal photo was the top of her head.

One might have argued the girl's purposefully disappeared but the bones say otherwise. The two Dutch men in the village having an early lunch with them that day were never identified. Could they have been more involved?

Did a local stumble upon the bodies and use the camera's flash to see what had gone down, then became scared, and threw the backpack away? It is perhaps a sad ending that we may never truly know exactly what happened to Kris and Lisanne.

And so I ask you the question. What's more likely, that two Dutch travellers went into a jungle unprepared and suffered an accidental death, or that they were murdered by a creepy guide, cannibal tribe, or human traffickers?

After all the discussion above, there is one final spanner to throw into the works. One that many researchers could never really fathom and still struggle to comprehend. Kris's bones were not white because of natural weathering – they had been chemically cleaned.

Bizarre True Crime enters double digits with Volume 10.

OUT NOW!